THE
GOD
Positioning
System

LEROY BANKS

ISBN 979-8-89345-046-0 (paperback)
ISBN 979-8-89345-047-7 (digital)

Christian Faith Publishing
832 Park Avenue
Meadville, PA 16335
www.christianfaithpublishing.com

Printed in the United States of America

CONTENTS

INTRODUCTION

God Positioning System

There are times when I pray and pray, and it seems like God is silent. It seems as if I am never going to get the answer. Then there are times when I am doing things that are not spiritual, and God speaks. I can be exercising and listening to gospel music. Not trying to be spiritual, just trying to use music to pass the time and keep my mind off how tired I am. Suddenly, out of nowhere, God speaks to me. There are times I am sitting in a class, not a Sunday school or theology class. It could be a work class or a college course, and suddenly God speaks through something that the instructor says to the class. There are times when I am driving to the store or someplace, not expecting a word from God, but you guessed it; God speaks.

One morning as I was headed to work, I ran into traffic. I was late for work that day. The boss that I had at that time lived in the same city as me. We had about the same drive to work. However, he made it to work on time. If he made it on time, I should have made it on time. At least that is how the logic works out in my mind.

In a meeting later that day, we were all talking about the morning traffic and how long it took us to get to work. My boss said that his GPS took him in a different way than normal. It directed him around the traffic, and he was able to make it to work on time. My car is not equipped with GPS, but that is not an excuse. I have a smartphone, and as we all know, there is an app for that.

I started turning on my GPS every morning so that it could direct me around any accidents or traffic problems. The GPS would direct me around, and I would get to work on time. Even on those mornings when there were accidents blocking the road, the GPS would lead me in the right direction. Most of the time it was no big deal; the roads would be clear. On those mornings, the GPS directed me to go the way I normally go.

God began to speak to me based on things the voice on the GPS would say. Things like "You are on the fastest route," or "There is heavier traffic than normal." At first it was just a sermon, but then I heard the voice of God telling me to write this book.

CHAPTER 1

The Road to Destiny

I knew you before I formed you in your mother's
womb. Before you were born, I set you apart and
appointed you as my prophet to the nations.

—Jeremiah 1:5

A few months ago, my wife and I were trying to find a graduation
celebration for a young man from our church. We drove up the
road, and the address numbers started getting too high. We turned
around and drove back the way we came, and then the address numbers started getting too low. We turned around again and started
driving, and suddenly, the address numbers were getting too high
again. We turned around again. Finally, my wife saw a balloon and
said, "There it is." We finally knew where to make the next turn to
get to the celebration.

We had to make a turn onto a little one-lane side road, and the
house was about a quarter mile off the main road we were driving on.
When we started out, we knew where we wanted to go. We wanted
to get to a graduation celebration. However, we did not know exactly
how to get there. Many times, our walk with Christ is just like that.
We have a vision of where we want to go. We have a desire to get to
where God is leading us, but we are not exactly sure how to get there.

We don't know how to bring to pass the assignment, but the great thing is, there is someone who does know how to get there. That person is the Holy Spirit. We must allow the Holy Spirit to lead us throughout this journey. We needed a balloon to show us the next turn for the celebration, but in this spiritual journey that we are on, the Holy Spirit is so much better than a balloon. The Holy Spirit will show us the road to make the next turn onto. When we follow the leading of the Holy Spirit, each road we go down will bring us closer to our destiny. For us, it was just one balloon that day, but in this life, we may have many turns and many roads to go down. The Holy Spirit will lead us down each road we must take.

Jeremiah 1:5 says, "I knew you before I formed you in your mother's womb. Before you were born, I set you apart and appointed you as my prophet to the nations." Let's just focus on the word *knew* for a moment. The first thing we see is that *knew* means "to perceive and see." Before God formed us in the womb, He could already see where He wanted us to be in this life. God could see the ministry that He called us to. I was twenty-four years old when I was filled with the Holy Spirit. God saw that day before I was born. I pray that each of us will understand that God allowed us to go down the roads we went down because there was something that we needed on that road. There was something or someone we needed to pick up on that road, or there was something or someone you needed to drop off on that road. All of it was working so that God could get you to the place where He saw you before you were born.

Knew also means "to be acquainted with." If you and I want to get acquainted with one another, we would have to spend time with one another. We would have to talk to one another. We would have to listen to one another. It would take time for us to truly get to know each other's likes and dislikes. The God whom we serve, on the other hand, was acquainted with us before He formed us in the womb of our mothers. He knew everything about us, before He formed us in the womb. Of course, we were not acquainted with Him at this point. He already knew every bad decision we would make and every wrong road we would go down. Still, He loves us so much that He still ordained us with purpose.

He knows us, and He knows what He has called us to do. This is why it is so important to seek Him on this journey. When we seek the kingdom of God, He has promised to give us everything we need. One of the things we need is divine direction for our purpose in Jesus. When we seek the kingdom of God first, the direction we should go in our life will come. He will not just give us direction, He will also give us the wisdom that we need to move forward in the right direction. When we seek the kingdom of God first, He will direct us and guide us on the road to our destiny.

Many of us have asked questions like, *How do I find out what God wants me to do? Why has God called me to the kingdom for such a time as this? How do I find my purpose?* Purpose is defined as the reason for which something is done, created, or exists. Many of us in this life are trying to find out why we were created. Can I go to a teacher, a pastor, a mentor, or councilor to find why I was created? God can use one of them to give some good advice, but if we really want to find why we were created, we need to seek the Creator. When we seek the Creator and His righteousness above all other things, even the reason we exist will be added. It is God's desire that we are on the right road to reach our destiny in Him. He is the author and finisher of our faith, and He wants us on the right road. The only way we can find purpose is through the one who gives purpose.

James 1:5 (NLT) says, "If you need wisdom, ask our generous God, and He will give it to you. He will not rebuke you for asking." God will not only give you direction, He will give you the wisdom that you need to operate in your ministry. God will give you skill in the management of affairs pertaining to your ministry, business, marriage, and on and on. God wants His people to have wisdom. God wants His children to have the skills they need to manage the affairs of the kingdom. This is so important because the wisdom on the kingdom is different from the wisdom of this world. The wisdom of this world will say, "Get ahead by any means necessary." The wisdom of the kingdom says, "Don't trust the wisdom of the world." The wisdom of the kingdom will tell us to trust in the Lord with all our heart and lean not to our own understanding. It is God's desire is to give us the wisdom we need to understand and walk in our purpose. All we need to do is ask and listen to what God is speaking to us. Then we need to follow the direction that He gives.

There are so many ways that can help us with navigation today. We have navigation apps on our cell phones, iPads, and tablets. Many cars today have GPS. The GPS will give us the directions, but we have to listen and follow the directions. There have been many occasions when I would turn the GPS but not listen to what it was saying. I did not like the direction it was telling me to go. I already knew the way home, so I just ignored the directions. I turned it on to lead me down the fastest route, but I did not listen.

I was hearing what the GPS was saying, but I was not following the directions that it gave me. I wanted to do what I wanted to do. I wanted to go my own way and do my own thing. I wanted to go the familiar way. I had set the address to my home in the GPS. That means the GPS knew where I was going before I started driving. The GPS knew where my destination was located. It also knew where I was in relationship to my destination. The GPS could see all that was going happening on all the roads between my job and my home. Still, day after day, I would turn on the GPS. Day after day, it would try to put me on the fastest route. Day after day, I did not listen. I did what I thought was best.

> "My thoughts are nothing like your thoughts," says the Lord. "And my ways are far beyond anything you could imagine. For just as the heavens are higher than the earth, so my ways are higher than your ways and my thoughts higher than your thoughts." (Isaiah 55:8–9 NLT)

This is a powerful scripture for us. We all have thoughts of how we think our lives and should be. We all have thought of how we think we can best reach our destination. The problem is that God does not think the way the human mind thinks. There may be roads that He wants us to walk down that the person before us did not have to walk. There may be circumstances and situations that we have the walk through that someone else did not have to walk through. God knows that best way for each of us to get to our destiny.

The problem each day was not the GPS. The problem was me. I wanted the GPS to lead the way I wanted to go. I wanted the GPS to think like I think. The GPS, on the other hand, had a better view than I had. The GPS could see things that I was not aware of. It is the same in our walk with God. We have to realize that He may not be leading us the way we want to go, but He is all-seeing, and He is all-knowing. We have to make the decision that we are not going to be led by our flesh. We must be led by the Spirit. I'm not talking about the global position system; I'm talking about the God position. The Holy Spirit is our God Positioning System.

There finally came a day when I decided I was going to listen to the GPS no matter what it said. If it said turn left, I was going left. If it said right, I was going to turn right. It did seem to me that a left turn was the wrong way. By the time I get off in the afternoon, there is a lot of traffic on the roads. Many times, the GPS would take me on some back roads. Many times, I thought this phone is going to lose service while I'm in the middle of nowhere. The one thing I did not want to do was lose my connection.

In our walk with Christ, we should always desire to keep our connection to Him. It may seem like we are on a long dark road sometimes, but if God has us on that long dark road there is a purpose behind it. There are many times in my life when I don't understand things right away, but down the line, the Lord shows me why I needed to go through a particular test or trial. He shows me what He put in me or what He took out of me during the test. Then He helps me understand why it was so important. Without God, we will never reach our true potential. Our connection with God must be the most important connection in our lives. When all else fails, we must maintain the connection to God. If you don't get anything else out of this book, please get this: stay connected to God.

There have been times in my life that I have applied for jobs and did not get them. It was not a good feeling. There have been times in my life when I have prayed, and things did not go the way I expected them to go. Through it all, I stayed connected to God.

Eventually I would see why that was not the right job, or why the prayer was not answered in the way expected. Romans 8:28 let us know that "all things work together for good to them that love God, to them who are the called according to His purpose." Maintain the connection and see how God turns every situation in your favor.

I worked in security for many years. I can honestly say that I strongly disliked that job. Especially in the winter. I do not like being out in the cold. I like it warm and toasty year-round. My dislike for this job was the reason I went to college to be a BA degree. Many of the things I was taught in those courses are helpful to me today. But I have to say this: my degree did not get me my current job. It was the grace of God that put me in this position. By man's standards, I'm not qualified for my current job, but with God on my side, I make it from day today.

Jeremiah 29:11 (NLT) says, "For I know the plans I have for you," says the Lord. "They are plans for good and not for disaster, to give you a future and a hope." Those days I spent in security was not because God had plans to make me suffer for a few years. Eleven years, three months, and three weeks to be exact. It was just after September 11, 2001, that I was hired into security. When most jobs were laying off, security was hiring. God used that security job to take care of my family; to keep a roof over our head, food on the table, clothes on our backs, and shoes on our feet. It may not have been what I wanted, but it was what I needed. I showed up and did the job to the best of my ability. That security job was a blessing to me and my family on many levels. God knew exactly what He was doing. He gave me a future and a hope. It did not seem like it at the time, but God's way is the best way.

In the medical field, they have what is called a central line. A central line is like an intravenous (IV) line. But it is much longer than a regular IV and goes all the way up to a vein near the heart or just inside the heart. God desires to be our central line today. He wants to speak directly to our hearts. He wants to put the things that are in His heart directly into our hearts. God wants to impart directly into our lives. I'm glad that God has given us prophets and others to speak into our lives, but I'm also thankful that He speaks directly to us. Through the power of the Holy Spirit, we can hear God for ourselves. We can hear Him speak anywhere and anytime. God is not just a pulpit speaker. God is not just a Sunday morning speaker. God will speak to His people all day, every day. We need to take God out of the pulpit box we have Him in and allow ourselves to hear Him speak to us seven days a week. Let Him reveal His plan for our lives. Plans for a future and a hope.

We have a choice. We can choose to follow the Lord on the road to our destiny, or we can choose another road. There are many roads that we can choose to travel on in this life, roads like the road of hurt and the road of pain. We can choose the road of anger and jealousy. We can choose the road of doubt and fear.

The road of hurt and pain is a road that leads to nowhere. It just goes around in circles, revisiting the places where someone or something caused us pain. The pain and the hurt have a hold on us, and it is hard to let go. We should never stay on the road of hurt and pain. If we do, it will lead us to the road of anger and bitterness. A road that we don't want to travel.

There is the road of doubt and fear. If only we could see ourselves the way God sees us. If only we knew that things about ourselves that God knows. When we are born in Christ, He sees the new creature. If we could see what God sees, we would have no doubt of what He could use us to do. If we could see what God sees in us, all fear would be gone. We can't see what God's sees, but we can trust that He has us on the right path and step out.

I truly believe that each day of our lives, God's presence goes before us and behind us. I believe that He dwells inside us and all around us. God wants us to lie down in green pastures, and God wants to lead us beside the still waters. It is His desire to make our way prosperous. The question that we must ask ourselves is, will we trust Him? Will we say the words *I trust You, Jesus, with every area of my life*?

CHAPTER 2

The Correct Address

The LORD directs the steps of the godly. He delights in
every detail of their lives. Though they stumble, they will
never fall, for the LORD holds them by the hand.

—Psalms 37:23–24

There are times when I must go to an appointment at a place
where I have never been before. There are times when I want
to attend a service at a church I have never attended before or don't
attend very often. Back in the day, my wife and I would print out
directions online. I would drive, and she would give me step-by-step
instructions. Turn left here, turn right at the next light, and so on.
Now we just put the address in the GPS on one of the smartphones
in the car. The GPS then gives step-by-step directions on how to get
where we are going. One of the important things in this process is to
put the correct address into the GPS. For us to get to the right place,
we had to put in the correct address.

When we apply this concept to our walk with God, we want
to go to the place where God desires for us to go. There is no better
place to be than where God wants us to be. Without a doubt, the
wrong address will take you someplace. The wrong address may even
take you to a nice place that feels like a spiritual place. The wrong
address may take you to a place where you seem to be prosperous. As

great as the wrong address might seem, the wrong address will not take you to the right place.

There will be many people in our lives who think that they can give us the correct address on where to go in life. Many people along the way will tell us what they see in us. Many will try to tell us what God has called us to be. What other people see in us is not as important as what God sees in us. The Bible tells us that the steps of the righteous are ordered by the Lord. No man or woman can give us what must come from God. The only one who can give us the right address is Jesus.

An address is defined as the specifics of the place where someone lives or an organization is situated. An address can also be defined as a string of characters that identifies a destination for email messages or the location of a website. When God created us, He gave us a string of characters, or I should say characteristics, that were design to get us to the correct address. When we accept who God called us to be and where God called us to be, we will experience great rewards.

Teachers are great, and they are greatly needed in our lives. Teachers can speak into our lives, and teachers can help us learn more about this spiritual journey that we are on. Teachers, however, did not create us, and they cannot give us the correct address for God's purpose in our lives. Pastors are also great men and women. They pray over us, mentor us, preach to us week after week. The pastor still cannot give you your God-given assignment. Your God-given assignment must come for God. I'm not saying that God cannot use a pastor or teacher. The assignment can't come from them; it must come for God.

There are many other people in our lives with various titles who will tell us who we are and what we are. Friends, family, and acquaintances all see things in us. But remember the Bible in 1 Corinthians 13:9: "Now our knowledge is partial and incomplete, and even the gift of prophecy reveals only part of the whole picture!" We don't see the whole picture. God sees all and knows all. We must go to God.

God created us on purpose, with purpose, and God knows the exact ministry, business, and church that He has called us to. That tells me, if I want to know what direction I should take, I need to look to Jesus. Jesus will show us the right direction to go if we want to move toward our divine purpose. I have heard stories of how my pastor in the early days of the church would talk about building a community center. It did not happen right away. However, since he knew what God had called him to do, he was able to stay on course. He knew his God-given assignment. He knew the right address. I can imagine that it was not always easy. But today, that community center stands as a testimony of God's faithfulness.

This is the kind of example that we should follow. We should allow God to download the correct address into our spirit. Once we have the address, we must allow Him to guide us every step of the way, one step at a time, until we reach the address. Some roads will be smooth and easy. Other roads will be rough and rugged. No matter what the road is like, stay the course until you arrive.

When my wife and I moved back to Port Orchard, I programmed the address into the GPS on my phone. I wanted to make sure I was driving home the fastest way each day after work. However, the GPS always wanted to give me crazy directions at the end. It would want me to turn right when I needed to turn left. Then it would want me to pass by the house and go to the end of the street and make another turn. After a while, I got tired of this. I looked at the GPS to see what the problem was. The problem was I had programmed in the wrong address for home. I had the right street but the wrong number. The GPS was taking me to the address that I had programmed. The wrong address took me to the wrong place.

The wrong place may not be a bad place, but it is still the wrong place. Being on the choir is a good place, but God has called you to the usher board. Being on the deacon board is good, but God has called you to preach. There are a lot of good things that we can do, but it is so much better when it's a God thing. When our steps are ordered by God, He will lead us to the things that He ordained for us long ago. Ephesians 2:10 says, "For we are God's masterpiece." He has created us anew in Christ Jesus, so we can do the good things He planned for us long ago. He knows the address. All we have to do is ask Him for it.

Keeping in mind that we do not set the address; we must be careful about our ideas. We see another person doing something and having success. We want to experience that same success. We put a plan together to do what we saw that person doing. We don't take time to ask God if it is His plan. We put a plan together, and we are off to the races. We just ask God to bless our plan. We even find scripture to back it up. Psalms 1:3 says, "They are like trees planted along the riverbank, bearing fruit each season. Their leaves never wither, and they prosper in all they do." Instead of trusting God with the address, we ask God to take us to the address that we have decided on and put it above the address He has for us.

Moving toward the correct address in God involves trust. When we put our trust in God, sometimes it may seem like He is taking us in the wrong direction. God's thoughts are not our thoughts; His ways are not our ways. Sometimes it can seem like God is leading us to the wrong address because things don't look like we thought they would look. The next turn is not where we thought it would be. We thought we would be at the next level by now. What we thought we would be doing is not what God is leading us to. The question is, will we have the strength to say, "Lord, not my will but Your will be done"? In these times, we still must trust that God knows what He is doing and where He is leading.

There are times when I'm driving and listening to the GPS on my phone. It feels like the GPS is taking me in the wrong direction. I do not like that feeling. I do not know where the next turn will be, and I don't recognize the landscape. Sometimes the road seems to be in the middle of nowhere. This can't be the right way, I think. Then all of a sudden, I would see something that I recognized. When we stay God's course, He will get us there. Even though it did not look right in my mind, the GPS was taking me in the right direction. We may not see a familiar landscape for a while on this journey, but trust God. He has us headed in the right direction. His view is much better than our view. He sees parts of the road we never knew existed.

Trust in God and lean not to our own understanding. When we put our trust in Him, He will get us to the correct address. To trust means to be confident or sure. As I have grown in Christ over the past twenty-plus years, I have learned to have confidence in His ability to bring me out. That confidence has come through seeing all the things He has done in my life. That confidence comes through listening to the testimony of others. Many of those testimonies come from people who are not saved, but they knew enough to call on the name of Jesus in their time of trouble. If people who don't have a relationship with God can trust Him, then surely, we who have a relationship with Him can trust Him. That confidence should only grow through the experiences of seeing God work in our life and the lives of others.

In my walk with God, trust has not always been easy. It was difficult to step out in faith the first few times. Even now, it is not the easiest thing to do. I have found that I need to spend more time in His presence. I have found that I need to spend more time in His Word. I have found that I need to spend more time in prayer. The more time I spend in communion with Him, the easier it becomes to trust Him in every area of my life. Romans 10:11 tells us, "Anyone who trusts in Him will never be disgraced."

Let me give a testimony from early in my marriage. I was a young husband growing in faith. My wife and I had an electric bill that was well over a hundred dollars. All we had was about fifty dollars. The Holy Spirit told me to put the fifty dollars in offering that Sunday morning. This did not make sense to me at all. We had paid our tithes already. I'm going to church expecting God to lead someone to give us the rest of the money to pay the bill. Instead, God tells us to give what we have to the church. Out of obedience, we gave the fifty dollars that we had. We did not know how it would work out. All we could do was trust. A day or two later, we received a check in the mail for more than enough to pay the electric bill. That is the God that we serve. We must have the kind of trust in God that will allow us to step out in His Word.

The Word of God says in John 10:27, "My sheep hear my voice, and I know them, and they follow me." We must learn to distinguish between all the voices of the world and the voice of God. We must make sure we are not moving by our flesh. The flesh is against God and therefore cannot be trusted. We can always trust the leading of the Lord. He loves us so much that He gave His only begotten Son. He will not lead us astray.

God always knows what we need, and He knows when we need it. Today, as we sat in church, there was a powerful word. It was on the confession of faith. I began to confess that I can do all things through Christ who strengthens me. We all need the confession of faith that we will trust the Lord.

I was sitting in a minister's meeting one Sunday morning. The training for that morning was on tithes and offering. I asked a question to the elder who was teaching. I said there are so many Christians who give so much and still struggle. Why are all the faithful givers not rich? The elder's response was "Obedience." If we want to truly experience the blessing of God, giving is not enough. There must be obedience along with giving. When God gives the direction to start a business, write a book, start a ministry, or put in for that promotion, we must be obedient.

We are looking for blessing to come in one way. Many times, the blessing we are seeking does not come the way we are thinking. The blessings will come in the form of a God idea. When that God idea comes, be obedient. The courage and obedience to step out and follow God's direction will get you to the correct address. The road to our destiny requires obedience.

I taught the youth Sunday school class, and often I would tell them, "You were born at just the right time to do what God wants you to do." It is not a mistake that we were born at the time we were born. God planted us in the right family, the right state, and the right city. He knows what it will take to give us the tools that we need.

Yes, we will make mistakes along the way, but nothing that happens in my life is a surprise to God. He knows the accidents and traffic problems that will be on the road in my life, and He knows the trials and tribulations that I must endure. I have to keeping listening and be willing travel the uncomfortable road.

"Trust in the Lord with all thy heart" means that we absolutely rely upon God's wisdom, power, and goodness. When we trust in the Lord with all our heart, there is no doubt. There is no room for flesh to come in and create doubt when we are trusting in God with all our heart.

What is it *all thy heart*? *All* is defined as the whole of one's energy or interest. This says to us that when we trust God with all our heart, all our energy goes toward trusting Him. There is no energy left for doubt. There is no energy left for fear. All our energy is put into trust. The God that we serve deserves our trust.

Next is interest. We should only be interested in things that cause us to trust in the Lord. In order to get there, we have to stay in His word, and we have to continue in prayer. We should listen to the testimony of those who trusted Him and see the results of their trust. When we trust in God, our trust will be rewarded. He will lead us to the right address.

The correct address has been or will be downloaded into us at the appointed time. When the right address has been given, when we know the way should be traveling, the person who follows the directions is the person who will have joy, unspeakable joy. The person who follows the directions will step on the devil's head. The person who follows the directions is the person who will impact this world for the kingdom of God. Let God lead you to the correct address.

CHAPTER 3

Listen to the Directions

For I know the thoughts that I think toward you, saith the LORD,
thoughts of peace, and not of evil, to give you an expected end.

—Jeremiah 29:11

I can remember times when I would be driving home listening to
the GPS. The GPS would start to take me in a certain direction,
and I think, *I know exactly where you are going to take me.* Since in my
mind I already know where to go, I stop paying so much attention to
what the GPS is saying. I get to a light, and the GPS says turn left,
but I'm in the lane to go straight. There is traffic in the turn lane,
and I didn't want to hold up the people behind me. I ended up going
the wrong direction because I stopped listening and thought I knew
where to go next.

We can take that same approach with God. *This route looks
familiar to me. I got this. I know exactly what God is going to say next.*
Instead of listening carefully for the next step, we move out on our
way of thinking. We think we got this figured out; no more direction
needed. This is a big mistake. We should never move out on our way
of thinking. I say that again: we should never move out on our way
of thinking. We must be led by God.

The Bible tells us that the heart or mind of man is desperately
wicked. Many times, we think we have the best intentions, but deep

down inside, there is something else driving the decision. There is a selfish motive behind it all. For example: I'm supporting you to get into office because I think you are the best candidate. However, deep down inside, the truth of the matter is, I support you for office because of what I think you will do for me once you are elected. I see some contracts coming my way. I see a promotion coming my way. I see money coming my way. I see status coming my way. I think my motives are pure, but deep down, it's all about me.

This is why it is so important that when God has us on an assignment we not follow our own thinking. Jeremiah 29:11 says, "For I know the thoughts that I think toward you, saith the LORD, thoughts of peace, and not of evil, to give you an expected end." Jeremiah wrote this to his brothers and sisters who were exiled in Babylon. It was given to him by God to encourage them in the fact that God had a plan.

I know that God's plan was not their plan. Their plan would have been for God to destroy the Babylonians. Their plan would have been for God to release them from captivity right away. God's plan said for them to build homes and plan to stay in captivity. God's plan said to get married and have children in captivity. God's plan said to plant gardens in captivity. God's plan said, "You are staying here for seventy years." For some, that meant they would die in captivity. We have to have the mindset that it is better to die in captivity if it is God's plan than to walk around in freedom in our plan.

As I think about how I would get a few directions from the GPS and then think I did not need any more assistance, I wonder if I take that same approach in my relationship with God. I wonder how often my thoughts lead me away from the plan that God has. How often do I stop listening to God's directions?

In 1 Kings 19, when God told Elijah to go out and stand before Him on the mountain, we notice that God was not in the wind, the earthquake, or the fire. Exodus 19:18 says, "All of Mount Sinai was covered with smoke because the LORD had descended on it in the form of fire. The smoke billowed into the sky like smoke from a brick kiln, and the whole mountain shook violently." We see here that the Children of Israel had experienced God's presence in the earthquake and fire before. Second Samuel 22:11 says, "Mounted on a mighty angelic being, he flew, soaring on the wings of the wind." We see here they had experienced God's presence in the wind before. As Elijah stood on the mountain, he most likely expected the wind, the earthquake, the fire, or something like that to happen. The way God came had to be a real surprise to the man of God. What a wonderful surprise for God to speak in a still, small voice.

God is not always going to come in the way you want Him to come. God is not always going to speak in the way you think He is going to speak. Know this, people of God. God is speaking. He is giving us direction day by day. Are we so distracted by the way we think He is coming that we can't see how He truly is coming? Are we so distracted by the way we think He is going to speak that we can't hear when He does speak?

I want to take the fastest way home each day, so I turn on the GPS, but once I think I got it figured out, I stop listening for the way I need to take. In our walk with Christ, we want things to happen quickly, but there is usually traffic. The church that God said to start is not growing like you think it should grow. That ministry that God said to start up is not taking off the way you think it should. That business that God directed you to build has not prospered the way you imagined it would happen. It is during these times that we can get frustrated and want to give up.

The church should be a megachurch by now. The Word is good. Praise and worship is good. Good programs and ministries are going forth. It's a good ministry doing great things for the community. It should be getting get a lot more support and grants. Other businesses are growing and flourishing, with customers and clients coming and going daily. Seeing all this, some may want to give up. Don't give up but follow the directions laid out by God. Nothing that happens in our lives has taken God by surprise. He has a plan.

Jeremiah 29:11 says "thoughts of peace, and not of evil, to give you an expected end." God did not say thoughts for it to happen quickly. He said thoughts of peace. God did not say thoughts for it to happen according to man's schedule. God said thoughts to give you an expected end. There is a plan. The things that God is allowing to happen is not for evil. He is allowing you time to prepare for what He is going to do. God has an expected outcome for your assignment.

Listening to the directions that God gives can be hard sometimes. After all, God thinks differently than we think. God says it is more blessed to give than to receive. If you ask most people, they will say it is more blessed to receive than to give. They would say when they give, they have less, but when they receive, they have more. That makes perfect sense to me. God, on the other hand, knows what He will do in the life of a giver. The fact the God gives it back in good measure, pressed down, shaken together, and running over, it is more blessed to give.

To listen very simply means to give one's attention. When we say that we are listening to God, we are saying that we are giving Him our attention. With all the thing in the world that try to pull our attention away from God, we need to be intentional about giving Him our attention. There are times when I'm playing music, and it makes it hard to hear the directions from the GPS. The GPS and the music are playing from the phone. If I turn the music down, I also turn the GPS down. What I must do is turn the music off and leave the GPS on. Then all the speaking is the GPS. I can hear it clearly. We need to turn off all the distractions in our life and spend time with God getting directions each day.

Direction is defined as the management or guidance of someone. God wants to guide us along this journey. The church has fifty members. God wants to guide the church to a hundred. The business is making a hundred thousand dollars a year. God wants to give guidance to get to two hundred thousand. When we are in the valley of decision, God wants to give us guidance. It does not cost any money. All we must do is listen. We need to open our spiritual ears to hear what the Lord is saying for the season that we are in.

Now, God never promised that we would not experience storms in this life. When we are in the midst of the storm, it can seem like the storm is lasting for a while. Remember, a quick delivery was not promised, but there is a promise of a plan. The storm has a purpose. Keep listening to God, and He will show you how to navigate through the storm. You will be stronger when you come out on the other side.

The plan is laid out, and we must choose to follow the directions given by God. When we look ahead, we may just see the next few steps we need to take. God sees every step we need to take all the way to victory. By faith, take those next few steps. As God continues to guide, take the next few steps after that. Sometimes it may be an uphill battle to take the next step, but keep on stepping. There will be times when the next step seems like walking through the fire. First Peter 1:7 says, "These trials will show that your faith is genuine. It is being tested as fire tests and purifies gold—though your faith is far more precious than mere gold." When your faith remains strong through many trials, it will bring you much praise and glory and honor on the day when Jesus Christ is revealed to the whole world. Keep stepping in the direction God is leading.

God has a plan. A plan is a detailed proposal for doing or achieving something. God has every detail laid out. All we must do is follow the directions. I'm a manager at my job, and I make a lot of mistakes as I manage. However, when God is managing, there are no mistakes. We must get to a place in God where we can say, "Lord, thank You for the test. I know there is a plan. Lord, thank You for this storm. I know there is a plan."

The GPS gives directions when it is time to turn left or right. It gives direction when you need to keep straight. It gives directions when it is time to take an exit off the highway, and it gives directions when it is time to merge onto the highway. The same way it is with our God. He is giving directions all the way. When your business gets to this level, do this. When your church grows to this many members, do this. Now is the time to move to a new building, buy some land, and build a new building. Sometimes, the direction may be to hold fast. But be obedient, and you will reap the blessings.

It is amazing how easily I get to where I'm going when I listen to the directions. I know in the end I want to be at a church building or some type of office building. I just don't know each turn to make along the way. However, if I listened to the GPS, I would get there. My wife and I can drive from Port Orchard, Washington, on the West

Coast of the US to Denmark, South Carolina, on the East Coast. If we follow the directions, we will get there. On the other hand, if we do not listen to the directions, we could end up on any random road or street anywhere in the US. We don't want to be delayed getting to our destination. We want to arrive at the appointed time.

Seeking direction from God is key to living a good Christian life and walking in the purpose that God has for us. Matthew 7:7 says, "Keep on asking, and you will receive what you ask for. Keep on seeking, and you will find. Keep on knocking, and the door will be opened to you." The word *seek* in Matthew 7 means "to crave." We should crave direction from God like we crave the food we eat. Crave direction from God as we start each day and throughout each day. Whenever we come to that proverbial fork in the road, it does not have to be a guess. We can be sure that we are going the right way when we seek direction from God. God can tell us which way to go, and He desires to tells us which way to go.

Matthew 7:8 should encourage us all the more. It says, "For everyone who asks, receives. Everyone who seeks, finds. And to everyone who knocks, the door will be opened." God does not limit His direction to just a select few people who seek, but everyone who seeks direction in God will find it. I look at it this way. When Leroy asks, he receives; when Leroy seeks, he finds; and when Leroy knocks, the door will be open. Every one of us should put our name in that scripture and trust that God will do what He says.

In Joshua chapter 9, the people of Gibeon heard what Joshua had done to Jericho. The people of Gibeon set out to deceive the Children of Israel. The Children of Israel examined the evidence with their eyes. In verse 14, we find that they did not seek the Lord. They trusted what they said. We never want to get to a place where we trust ourselves so much that we don't seek the Lord. In verse 16, three days after making the decision without direction from God, they find out the truth about the people of Gibeon. They find out that they had been deceived. There are many people in this world who will want to deceive us and pull us away from the plan that God has for us.

When we seek God, trust God and listen to the direction of God. He will give us the direction we need to make the correct decision. We never want to make the mistake that was made in Joshua 9. We want to continually seek God's direction. Not only to seek them but to listen to the directions. When we listen to the directions given by God, we will succeed in fulfilling our God-given assignment.

Proverbs 16:25 says, "There is a path before each person that seems right, but it ends in death." This verse is letting us know that we have a way in our heart that seems right. We have a direction we want to go that looks good to us, but when we follow our human minds, the path leads to death. The path we want to choose in the flesh will always be against the way God wants us to go. We must continually seek Him and the path that He desires for us.

Adam and Eve chose a way that seemed right unto them. Genesis 2:16–17 says, "But the LORD God warned him, 'You may freely eat the fruit of every tree in the garden except the tree of the knowledge of good and evil. If you eat its fruit, you are sure to die.'" God told them that they would die if they ate from the tree of knowledge of good and evil. They chose to go another way. They ate of the tree and died spiritually. They lost that close connection with God

We don't want to follow our own way of thinking. We want to follow the direction of God. If we listen to the directions given by God, we will reach our destiny. I say to each of you, listen to the directions.

CHAPTER 4

Headlights

Thy word is a lamp unto my feet, and a light unto my path.

—Psalms 119:105

In the late 1880s, the car was invented. Headlights were also invented around the same time. As you can imagine, both cars and headlights have greatly improved since that time. Headlights are used to illuminate the road in front of the car. Since the road in front of the car is illuminated, the driver can safely make it from point A to point B even at night. However, in order for the lights to illuminate the road, they must be on. If the lights are turned off at night, the driver drives in darkness. My question for you today is a very simple question. Is the light of God's Word turned off in your life?

I can remember when I first started driving. I would be driving during the day without headlights on. It would start getting dark over time, and I still would not have my headlights on. Soon, however, it would become very apparent that I needed to turn on the lights. At this point, I had a decision to make. Turn on the headlights or continue to drive around in darkness. I would choose to turn on the lights every time.

In Psalms 119, we read, "Thy word is a lamp unto my feet, and a light unto my path." As we move toward our destiny in God, we don't know every step to take. By the grace of God, we don't need to know every step to take. God has done something great for His people. He has given us His Word. He has also made His Word a lamp unto our feet and a light unto our path. I don't need to know the next step. I just need to know how to follow the Word of God.

Let's take a look at the first part of the scripture: *a lamp unto my feet*. Back in the Bible days, a lamp was more like a candle. But even if you think about the lamps we have today, they may light up the room that you are in, but the farther you get away from the light the darker it gets. This is why we carry the Word of God with us everywhere we go. As long as we are carrying the lamp, we can see our next step. As long as we are carrying the lamp, it will keep us from stepping into danger. There are many traps and snares that the enemy has set for us all along the way, but as long as we have our lamp, we can see them and avoid stepping on them. So many of God's people stumble and fall because they are not walking in His Word. We need our lamp.

Think about a big city like New York or Los Angeles. All the lights are on at night, lighting up these cities, but if a power outage happens, these cities are in the dark. Being without the Word of God is like being in a power outage. Without the Word of God, we are walking in the dark. When we can't see our way, that is when we stumble and fall. God's Word will show us the direction we should go. God's Word will keep us from tripping and falling. It is so important to stay in God's Word.

I want to share five of my favorite scriptures with you. Some people say they have one favorite scripture. Somehow, I cannot pick just one. There are many scriptures in the Bible that have helped me in my walk with Christ.

> Now unto him that is able to keep you from falling, and to present you faultless before the presence of his glory with exceeding joy, to the only wise God our Saviour, be glory and majesty, dominion and power, both now and ever. Amen.
> (Jude 24–25)

So shall they fear the name of the LORD from the west, and his glory from the rising of the sun. When the enemy shall come in like a flood, the Spirit of the LORD shall lift up a standard against him. (Isaiah 59:19)

He sent his word, and healed them, and delivered them from their destructions. (Psalms 107:20)

No weapon that is formed against thee shall prosper; and every tongue that shall rise against thee in judgment thou shalt condemn. This is the heritage of the servants of the LORD, and their righteousness is of me, saith the LORD. (Isaiah 54:17)

Trust in the LORD with all thine heart; and lean not unto thine own understanding. In all thy ways acknowledge him, and he shall direct thy paths. (Proverbs 3:5–6)

Then he answered and spake unto me, saying, this is the word of the LORD unto Zerubbabel, saying, Not by might, nor by power, but by my spirit, saith the LORD of hosts. (Zechariah 4:6)

As I was reading about headlights, I found out they have to be approved and not tampered with. We cannot tamper with the Word of God. We can't add to it, and we can't take from it.

Jesus replied, "You hypocrites! Isaiah was right when he prophesied about you, for he wrote, 'These people honor me with their lips, but their hearts are far from me. Their worship is a farce, for they teach man-made ideas as commands from God.' For you ignore God's law and substitute your own tradition." (Mark 7:6–8)

We also see this in Matthew 15:8–9.

Verse 7 says their worship is a farce. The King James Version uses the word *vain*. It means "fruitless." When we walk in our traditions as if they are the Word of God, our worship is fruitless. This means it is unsuccessful and produces nothing of value. We don't want our worship to be a farce. We want worship that produces much fruit. We want worship to draw us closer to God. To be clear, the traditions of men are not a lamp unto our feet. The Word of God is the lamp unto our feet. We need to ensure that we are following God's Word and not the traditions of men.

There was a time when we had to turn on the lights each time we would get into a car. Now there is a setting called auto. When we turn on the car, the lights automatically come on. When we are young in our walk with Christ, we may have to try look up scripture and try to find the right one for the situation we are dealing with. But the more we stay in the Word of God and the more we walk with Him, we will find the scripture becomes automatic. The scriptures are down inside of us. When we need them, the Holy Spirit will bring them to our remembrance. Then we have a light to help us to make the next step of our journey.

Headlights are designed to facilitate fatigue-free driving. When we think about fatigue, we think about energy, but there is another aspect of fatigue. Fatigue reduces the ability to do things and the ability to focus. The Word of God helps us to stay focused on the task at hand. We don't want to be out of focus spiritually.

A few years ago, I heard a lady say that the Bible should be rewritten to fit today. She doesn't understand that the Bible is written for today. God is the same yesterday, today, and forever. He does not change. The problem is that many people don't know how to apply the scripture today. Instead of applying God's Word with love, many apply it with judgment. John 13:34–35 says, "So now I am giving you a new commandment: Love each other. Just as I have loved you,

you should love each other. Your love for one another will prove to the world that you are my disciples."

The lamp unto our feet tells us that we are to take our next step in love. Then it tells us to take the step after that in love. When we are moving toward our God-given destiny, we are operating or stepping in love. If we are not operating in love, we are not operating in God. When we operate in the love of God, there is not a devil in hell that can stop us from accomplishing what He has called us to do.

Now let's take a look at *light unto my path*. As we walk in the world from day to day, we will be continuously faced with choices. The light unto our path helps us to make the right choices. When the world around us says that this is okay and that is okay, the light unto our path will give us the right direction. That light unto our path will lead us toward righteousness. The Word of God will show what is right, and the Word of God will help us to understand what is wrong. Then we can make wise decisions as we move forward.

The first acetylene lamps were actual flames. The flame had a mirror placed behind it. This was not very effective. Then came the electric headlight, and then sealed beam headlights. Headlights are still being improved to this day. The same way it is with God's Word. We may not be very effective in applying God's Word right away. We have to read and study and pray for understanding. Then as we grow in Christ, we will begin to understand more of His Word. Then we will be able to apply the Word of God in our lives. Second Timothy 2:15 says, "Work hard so you can present yourself to God and receive his approval. Be a good worker, one who does not need to be ashamed and who correctly explains the word of truth."

Hebrews 4:12 says, "For the word of God is alive and powerful. It is sharper than the sharpest two-edged sword, cutting between soul and spirit, between joint and marrow. It exposes our innermost thoughts and desires." The Word of God is not dead. The Word of God is alive. *Powerful* means the Word of God is active. The Word of God is active in our lives. When we read the Word, meditate on the Word, and speak the Word of God, we are speaking life, and we and the Word of God will be active.

The Word of God gives us wisdom. In 1 Kings 4:29, we read, "And God gave Solomon wisdom and understanding exceedingly much, and largeness of heart, even as the sand that is on the sea-shore." What did Solomon do? He asked. When we ask God for wisdom, He will give us wisdom also. As we read His Word and get closer to Him, we gain more and more wisdom to choose the right path each day.

The Word of God gives us joy. I can't tell you how many times my day has started out with joy because I started it out with the Word of God. When we read about the joy of Jesus, how can we not be encouraged? Hebrews 12:2 says, "We do this by keeping our eyes on Jesus, the champion who initiates and perfects our faith. Because of the joy awaiting him, he endured the cross, disregarding its shame. Now he is seated in the place of honor beside God's throne." Jesus was about to have nails driven through His hands and feet, be pierced in His side, whipped, punched, and slapped. He was able to look beyond His present situation and see His future with his Father in heaven. We also have a future in heaven with the Father, and that future far outweighs the present circumstances.

Romans 8:18 says, "Yet what we suffer now is nothing compared to the glory he will reveal to us later." This scripture should give us joy. Yes, we must go through some things in this life, but when we focus on Jesus, He is bigger than any problem we face. You lost your home to foreclosure, but you have a mansion waiting for you in heaven. You may be struggling to pay your bills, but there are no bills in glory. You may be sick in your body, but earth has no sickness that heaven cannot heal. When we allow the Word of God to get us into focus, we can have joy like no other.

I pray that God, the source of hope, will fill you completely with joy and peace because you trust in Him. Then you will overflow with confident hope through the power of the Holy Spirit. We serve God, the source of *all hope*. When we read this verse, we should have joy. If we trust Him, He will give us joy. No matter how things look, we must trust Him.

The Word of God gives us guidance. Psalms 25:9 says, "He leads the humble in doing right, teaching them his way." The Lord desires to lead His people in the way that they should go. The Lord knows that we will stumble and fall if we try to do things on our own. He does not want us to stumble and fall. He guides us along the way. If His Word does not guide us, we stumble around in darkness.

Psalms 23:2–3 says, "He lets me rest in green meadows; he leads me beside peaceful streams. He renews my strength. He guides me along right paths, bringing honor to his name." Peaceful streams or still waters is saying to us that God leads us to a peaceful place where we can rest in Him. He leads us to a place of peace where we can focus on His presence. The world all around us may be in chaos, but God will give us peace. The right path or the pathway of righteousness is telling us that God will lead in the kingdom way of doing things, not in the worldly way of doing things. Each day, read God's Word. He will give you the guidance that you need.

God's Word will change us or transform us. Romans 12:2 says, "Don't copy the behavior and customs of this world, but let God transform you into a new person by changing the way you think. Then you will learn to know God's will for you, which is good and pleasing and perfect." The Word of God will not allow us to stay as were prior to having a relationship with Him. God's Word will transform the way we think and the way we act. Challenge anyone to tell me you have been reading God's Word and His Word has not changed you. We may not be all the way there yet, but we have changed.

God's Word reveals Jesus to us. Colossians 2:9 reveals that He is the fullness of God: "For in Christ lives all the fullness of God in a human body." Matthew 1:23 reveals Him as God with us: "Look! The virgin will conceive a child! She will give birth to a son, and they will call him Immanuel, which means 'God is with us.'" John 11:25 reveals Him as the resurrection and the life. Jesus said, "I am the resurrection and the life. Anyone who believes in me will live, even after dying." John 14:6 reveals Him as the only way to the Father. Jesus said, "I am the way, the truth, and the life. No one can come to the Father except through me." I could go on and on about what the Word of God says about Jesus, but I challenge you to read the Word for yourself. Let the Word of God reveal Jesus to you.

The Word of God reveals the promises of God. We can stand on the Word of God. What He says will come to pass. Everything that He promised, He is going to do it. Deuteronomy 31:8 says, "Do not be afraid or discouraged, for the LORD will personally go ahead of you. He will be with you; he will neither fail you nor abandon you." When we are doing the will of God, He promises to go before us. What is God telling you to do? Go and do it. He has already gone before you and prepared the way. Not only does He promise to go before us, He also promises to not abandon or leave us. God is right there with us in the good times and the bad, the ups and the downs. You can count on the promises of God.

The Word of God is so powerful it would be impossible to list all the things that it does for us, but I want to mention one more thing. The Word of God feeds our spirit. This is so important for the Christian. What we feed gets stronger. If we feed the flesh, the flesh gets stronger. If we feed the spirit, the spirit the gets stronger. Matthew 24:24–25 says, "For false messiahs and false prophets will rise up and perform great signs and wonders so as to deceive, if possible, even God's chosen ones. See, I have warned you about this ahead of time." We need to feed our spirit so that we will not be deceived by the devil. The enemy wants to stop our purpose by any means. When we stay in the Word of God, feeding the spirit, we will not fall into the traps and snares of the enemy.

CHAPTER 5

You Are on the Fastest Route

But Samuel replied, "What is more pleasing to the LORD: your burnt offerings and sacrifices, or your obedience to his voice? Listen! Obedience is better than sacrifice, and submission is better than offering the fat of rams."

—1 Samuel 15:22

When I was growing up, we attended Capernaum Baptist Church in Denmark, South Carolina. As a kid, I did not understand or even pay attention to a lot of the teaching. One thing I did love about church was hearing the choir sing, especially the NA McNeil choir. We had another choir called the gospel chorus. They were a little older. Sometimes on Sunday morning, they would sing a song that said, "I'm on the right road now." I can't speak for everyone, but when traveling I want to be on the right road.

Sometimes when I'm driving home in the afternoon, I will hear the GPS say, "You are on the fastest route." It will say from time to time, "Traffic is slower than usual, but you are still on the fastest route." When starting a ministry or a business, not many people want to be on the slow road. We want things to happen fast. How fast can the ministry get to a hundred members? How fast can the business get to five hundred thousand dollars a year? We don't want the slow route; we want the fastest route.

The fastest refers to the quickest, most efficient way from point A to point B. One thing we must keep in mind is that the shortest route is not always the fastest route. There may be all kinds of conditions on the shortest route that will cause it to be the slowest route. As we travel from the start of the assignment to the end of the assignment, we want to optimize our time and resources. We want to be on the fastest route.

Here we go now. We have heard the voice of God say, go out and start a ministry, a business, or get a new job. By faith, we have stepped out on what we heard God say. By faith, we want to see what we have started move forward and prosper. What is it that makes my business, or my ministry, stand out? What is it going to take to see what we have believed? Did I really hear from God? These are the questions we begin to ask ourselves as we move forward in the call.

As I was thinking and praying about this chapter, I asked the Lord, "What is the fastest route?" What God revealed to me is that the fastest route is obedience. Obedience is simply compliance with an order, request, or law. Obedience is also submission to another's authority. In this case, I'm talking about submitting to the authority of God. As we read the Word of God, we will find many who walked in obedience.

The closer we are to Jesus, the more likely we are to be obedient. We must spend time with Jesus. The more time we spend with Him, the easier it will be to walk in obedience. Spending time with Him will build trust, and the more we trust Him, the more we will be willing to be obedient to Him. Take time each day with Him.

Influence is another factor in obedience. Influence is defined as the capacity to have an effect on the character, development, or behavior of someone or something, or the effect itself. How much capacity does Jesus Christ have in our lives to affect our character? How much capacity does Jesus have to affect our development? How much capacity does Jesus have in our lives to affect our behavior? How much influence does Jesus have in our lives? When we read the Word of God, does it influence us? When we come out of the prayer closet, have we been influenced by our time in prayer?

In the military, soldiers don't carry out missions on their own. However, when directed to carry out a mission by someone in authority, they carry out the mission to the best of their ability. This is how we must be in our relationship with God. God is not asking us to carry out our own missions. God is asking us to carry out missions that He planned for us long ago. We can see how the mission is going to turn out, but God already sees the end of the journey.

The Old Testament records the sacrifices that the Children of Israel made. There were burnt offerings (Leviticus 1, 6:8–13), grain offerings (Leviticus 2), peace offerings (Leviticus 7:11–21), sin offerings (Leviticus 4, Numbers 15), and trespass offerings (Leviticus 5:15). God wanted their obedience more than He wanted these sacrifices. The same is true today. God wants our obedience. Samuel 15:22 says obedience is better than sacrifice.

Deuteronomy 28:1–14 talks about the blessing of obeying the Lord and following all His commands. Some may argue that this is only for Israel, the seed of Abraham. Galatians 3:29 says, "And now that you belong to Christ, you are the true children of Abraham. You are his heirs, and God's promise to Abraham belongs to you." We are the spiritual seed of Abraham. I choose to believe that if we are obedient to Christ, all the blessings of Deuteronomy 28 belong to us.

I want to point out a few verses in Deuteronomy 28. Deuteronomy 28:3 lets us know that we will be blessed in the city and in the field. This scripture tells us that when we walk in obedience, we are blessed wherever we are. In the biggest city or the smallest little country town, wherever we are we have the blessing of God when we walk in obedience. Verse 6 lets us know that when we come into our home, we find that no evil has come upon our family members or our possessions. When we leave our home, God will make our way prosperous. We will be blessed as we go about our daily business.

Verse 7 lets us know that we may have enemies all coming against the same way. The enemy can line up as much as he wants to come against, but when we walk in obedience to the almighty God, we will see those enemies flee from us several different ways. We will have complete victory, and our enemies will scatter. Verse 12 talks about the good treasure of heaven. God is going to cause blessing to rain down on those who are obedient.

Many times in my life, I have chosen the road of disobedience. I can remember thinking this is not the right thing to do. I can remember at times thinking this is a bad decision, or I should not be doing this. Still the flesh would win the battle of the mind. This was not only before Christ, as expected, but also after coming to Christ. Thank God as I grow in Him this is happening less and less. The spirit is winning the battle more and more. I will say this. The road of disobedience did not lead to the results I thought it would lead to. When I follow the leading of the Holy Spirit, it always leads to good results. It may not be the results I expected, but God always has a plan.

I can remember times when I did not study as I should before teaching a Sunday school class. I knew I needed to study. The spirit was leading me to study, but the flesh wanted to watch TV or do something else, anything other than study. On Sunday when it was time to teach, I would be scrambling, and the class would not go too well. I would be watching the time, hoping for the class to be over soon. The weeks that I studied how and when the Holy Spirit was leading me to study, the class would be great. We would get into some lively discussion, comment after comment coming from the class. We would be laughing and having fun and breaking down the lesson. The time for class to end would come so quickly we would not finish the lesson for that week a lot of the time. That is obedience versus disobedience. Second Timothy 2:15 says, "Work hard so you can present yourself to God and receive His approval." Be a good worker, one who does not need to be ashamed and who correctly explains the word of truth.

There was a time when I bought this little red Mitsubishi. I did not feel right about buying this car. The price was right, and the car looked good, but it just did not feel right. I was working at the Kent facility at the time. It was a little over an hour's drive to work and back home. I think we all know how this story turned out. That car did not last very long at all. In a few months, my wife and I had to buy another car. I wanted to make sure God was in the process this time around. We sought guidance before going out to find a car. The car that we ended up buying lasted for years. That is obedience versus disobedience. Proverbs 3:6 says, "Seek his will in all you do, and he will show you which path to take."

I could go on and on. There were times when God wanted me to pray, and I did not pray or would pray quickly and try to move on to doing something else. There were times the Lord was saying, "Read the Bible," but I had something different in mind. Fasting is another good one. The flesh never wants to fast. The flesh always wants to fight against the leading of the Holy Spirit. I have learned that following the flesh will put me on a road to hell. Following the Spirit will put me on a road to eternal life.

First Peter 1:14 says, "So you must live as God's obedient children." Don't slip back into your old ways of living to satisfy your own desires. You didn't know any better then. Before we came to Christ, we made all sorts of decisions according to the flesh. We didn't know that these decisions were wrong at the time, but now that we have encountered Christ, we have a new way of doing things. Peter is warning us not to fall back into making decisions according to the flesh but to walk in obedience to the leading of God. The God that we serve is a holy God, and therefore, we must also be holy.

Acts 5:29 says, "We must obey God rather than any human authority." The apostles were dealing with the religious people of their day. The religious did not understand the call of God on their life. The religious wanted the apostles to stop doing what God was leading them to do. Even after being put in jail, the apostles chose to follow God.

We today need to follow the examples of the of the apostles. We need to obey God. When God is leading and guiding us, others may think that we are out of our minds. We must obey God. We will face opposition, but we must move forward in the name of Jesus. He will show us how to deal with the opposition. John 16:33 says, "I have told you all this so that you may have peace in me. Here on earth, you will have many trials and sorrows. But take heart, because I have overcome the world." God has already overcome all that we will go through.

When each of us looks at the assignment that God has given us, we find that the assignment is too great for us to do on our own. Many will get discouraged and stop right there. The assignment is supposed to be more than we can handle. God wants us to depend on Him. He wants us to walk by faith, but He does not want us to give up.

Abraham was obedient. Genesis 12:1 says, "The LORD had said to Abram, 'Leave your native country, your relatives, and your father's family, and go to the land that I will show you.'" It takes a great deal of obedience to leave and not know where you are going. Even though Abraham did not know where he was going, he trusted God to get him there. Abraham did one thing he was not supposed to do, and that was take Lot with him. God is a merciful God. He allowed Abraham the opportunity to correct this mistake. In Genesis, Abraham and Lot part ways.

In John chapter 9, Jesus heals a blind man using mud and obedience. After Jesus made the mud and put it on the man's eyes. Jesus then tells the blind man to go and wash himself in the pool of Siloam. The blind man was obedient to the directions that Jesus gave him. As a result, the blind man was healed. He was able to see after washing himself in the pool of Siloam.

When God bought the Children of Israel out of Egypt, they followed His leading. Numbers 9:18 says, "In this way, they traveled and camped at the Lord's command wherever he told them to go." Then they remained in their camp as long as the cloud stayed over the tabernacle. They moved with the cloud. We don't see a cloud today, but God is still leading. When we move with Him, we will succeed. They Children of Israel moved when it was time to move, but they camped when it was time to camp. When it was God's time, God led them into the promised land. Numbers 9:23 says, "So they camped or traveled at the Lord's command, and they did whatever the Lord told them through Moses." What is the command for you and me to do today?

Joshua 5:6 lets us know what happened to the men of Israel who did not obey God. The Israelites had moved about in the wilderness forty years until all the men who were of military age when they left Egypt had died, since they had not obeyed the Lord. For the Lord had sworn to them that they would not see the land He had solemnly promised their ancestors to give them, a land flowing with milk and honey. Don't allow disobedience to cause you to miss out on your promised land. Don't let fear, doubt, or anything else cause you not to step out in God's Word. God's Word is true and a solid foundation for us to stand on.

Their disobedience not only affected them, it caused all the Children of Israel to wander in the wilderness for forty years. An entire generation missed out on God's best. I don't want my disobedience to cause my family to miss out on what God has for us. I want my family to receive all of God best. The best of God comes with our obedience to His leading and guidance. Obedience is better than sacrifice. Choose obedience.

CHAPTER 6

Distracted Driving

And the cares of this world, and the deceitfulness
of riches, and the lusts of other things entering in,
choke the word, and it becometh unfruitful.

—Mark 4:19

Like most people, I have been guilty of distracted driving: looking at my cell phone, trying to change the radio, or doing something with the heat or air. One thing all these things have in common is that it takes my focus off the road. I can't say for sure, but I have heard that when glancing down at your phone, you can drive the length of a football field. That is a long way to drive without seeing where you are going. Many things could happen in that time. My definition of distracted driving is allowing anything or anyone to take our eyes or mind off the task of driving a car.

No one may die physically when we are distracted from our purpose in God, but people will die spiritually when we get distracted from our purpose. In Mark 4:19, Jesus talks about somethings that will get us distracted from His word. The first one is the cares of this world. Then the deceitfulness of riches. Then the lusts of other things. We will look at each of these and try to get a better understanding. We don't want to allow anything to come in and choke out the word that has been sown in our hearts.

The cares of this world refer to the people being drawn in a different direction. Let's take a look at a few examples of this. The preacher stands in the pulpit and delivers a powerful word on praying for the sick. You know someone in the hospital or at home sick. You feel the Holy Spirit speaking to you, saying go and pray for this person after service. All during the sermon, you are excited about the word. Then service ends. Someone reminds you that the football game is about to come on. You decide that you will try to go pray for the person after the football game. You have just been drawn into a different direction by the cares of this world.

Example 2. The preacher is preaching on giving, and God lays it on your heart to give a certain amount. The time comes to give. All of a sudden, you are reminded by the adversary that you have an old furnace and that you need to save that money just in case it goes out. You decide to tear up the check and keep your money in the bank. You have just been drawn away by the cares of this world.

Example 3. The Word of God came forth through the preacher, or even in a causal conversation with someone. The word reminds you of the importance of reading the Bible and praying. You decide that you are going to make time to pray and read the Bible daily. As soon as you sit down with the Word, the phone rings, and it's your buddy who you have not talked to in a long time. You decide to talk to your buddy. You have just been drawn in a different direction by the care of this world.

We cannot allow the cares of this world to distract us. Watching a football game is a nice, relaxing thing to do. Saving for a new furnace when you know yours is old and about to go out is wise. Reconnecting with an old buddy is also a good thing. They are all good things when done at the right time and don't interfere with what God is leading you to do. We must know what is good. We must know what is of God. God is always more important than good.

Next, we have the deceitfulness of riches. When something or someone is deceitful, it means they are guilty of or involving dishonesty. It also means they are false or misleading others. God does not have an issue with us being rich, but He does not want us to trust in our finances more than we trust in Him. The enemy wants us to trust in our bank accounts and material possessions more than we trust in our God.

The problem with trusting in riches is that all it takes is one major thing to go wrong in your life, and the riches are gone. My wife and I just had to pay for a new furnace and now the water heater. We paid almost a thousand dollars for plumbing issues, and now we need a new water heater. Our little savings account is getting smaller and smaller. It's not the saving that we are depending on; it is the blessing of the Lord. None of these things took Him by surprise, and He caused us to have what we needed.

The next thing that the enemy uses to distract us is the lusts of other things. *Lust* is defined as desire, a craving, or a longing (especially for what is forbidden). What the enemy does in many situations is take something that God made, which is good, and distorts it in the mind of mankind. It should not be a surprise to anyone that the enemy has taken sex and distorted it. God created it for marriage, to be enjoyed by husband and wife. The enemy has distorted it, and now more that 75 percent of people have sex before marriage. Many also have extramarital affairs. And it's not just sex—look at all the drugs that have a good purpose. Their purpose is to help heal, but the enemy has turned them from healing to addiction.

The enemy will use anything he can to distract us. He wants to choke the Word that is in us. The enemy does not want the Word to be fruitful. One thing that the enemy wants to use to distract us is social media. We can get caught up in trying to post everything about our lives and trying to read about everything that is going on in the lives of others. The next thing we know, it is time for bed. We have spent most of the day on social media. Time we could have spent in prayer, in the Word of God, or helping someone in need was spent online.

There is a lot of good that can come from social media. It makes it easier to keep up with family members. Instead of needed to contact each person individually, you can post an update on social media. It saves a lot of time. Social media can be used for ministry. There was a time when you had to pay a lot of money to be on TV to have a worldwide ministry. Now you get a social media platform and minster to people around the globe. College degrees can be completed online, and high schools are online now. Working from home—no problem now. All this good can be done with social media, but the enemy uses social media as a distraction, to keep us away from our purpose in God.

The enemy will use our career as a distraction. We need to make money to feed our families, to keep a roof over our heads and clothes on our backs. We need money to pay the electric bill and water bill and on and on. Some may not agree with me, but I believe vacations are essential. Vacations are not free. It takes money to go on vacation. The more money you make, the better life will be, right? The enemy will have us chasing promotions and working instead of going to church, getting up early in the morning, no time to pray and read the Word. Not wanting anyone to get in before us. Getting home at night too tired to read the Word and pray. No time for God while chasing that promotion.

I was thinking a little while back that I need to get a promotion or a second job. The Lord spoke to me so clearly and said, "The answer is not in a promotion or a second job. The answer is in obedience to what I have told you to do." When we walk in obedience to God, He will supply all our needs. David said it like this in Psalms 37:25: "Once I was young, and now I am old. Yet I have never seen the godly abandoned or their children begging for bread." I will trust in God and not my career. Don't let you career distract you from the assignment.

Relationships can be a distraction. Second Corinthians 6:14 says, "Don't team up with those who are unbelievers. How can righteousness be a partner with wickedness? How can light live with darkness?" I have seen it over and over. A believer gets into a relationship with an unbeliever, and the believer starts falling away from God. The relationship becomes a distraction. The unbeliever does not want to go to church; the unbeliever does not want godly fellowship. The unbeliever wants to get into activities that are not of God.

First Corinthians 15:33 says, "Don't be fooled by those who say such things, for bad company corrupts good character." Romantic relationships are not the only relationships the enemy will use to distract us. When we want to walk in our God-given assignment, the people we hang out with casually can be a distraction. People who have no focus for their life and are not trying do anything with their life will often not want to see anyone accomplish anything with their life. We want to be around people who inspire us to move forward. We can't let our relationships here on earth be a distraction to our relationship with our heavenly Father.

The enemy will want to use criticism as a distraction. Criticism is expressing disapproval of someone or something based on perceived faults or mistakes. I can remember being called into a meeting May or June 2022. The first question that was asked in the meeting was, "Leroy, who called you?" Time passed by, and I thought more and more about the question. I had served faithfully and had been walking in my calling for years. To hear my brothers and sisters ask me that question weighed on me more and more. It was as if they were saying, "We don't recognize God in your ministry." It was as if they were saying, "God didn't call you. Who called you?"

It is clear to me now that the enemy wanted to distract me. The enemy wanted me to give up, but the devil is a liar. In the name of Jesus Christ, I will not give up. Shortly after that meeting, the Lord led me to leave that ministry. I'm right where He wants me to be. What the enemy means for evil, God will use it for our good. I did not get here my way, but God did it His way. We cannot be distracted by what other people say about us. We must be concerned with what God says about us.

One other distraction I want to mention is negativity. Negativity is the inclination to be doubtful, downbeat, cynical, and disagreeable. When a person is negative, they tend to focus on what is going wrong and the worst possible outcomes. A person who is negative might say some things like "I tried this before. It did not work. Why should I waste my time trying again?" "I knew I should not have gone to the doctor. They always give me bad news." "God can't use me." If the enemy can get us focused on the negative, he can stop us in our tracks. Proverbs 4:23 says, "Guard your heart above all else, for it determines the course of your life."

We have to guard our minds against negativity. We must allow the Holy Spirit to lead and guide us toward gratefulness and thanksgiving. When we walk in thanksgiving, we can overcome the obstacles that the enemy put in our way. Thanksgiving will allow us to overcome negativity and move toward victory in Jesus. It is easy to not try when we believe we can't win. With God on our side, we will be victorious.

The distractions that I have mentioned are just the tip of the iceberg. There are many other distractions. There is debt, lies, temptations, persecutions, betrayal, and so many more. The enemy does not want us to accomplish anything for Jesus. He will bring distractions. The Lord, however, has given us weapons to combat the distractions of the enemy. Second Corinthians 10:3–5 lets us know that these weapons are not carnal, but they are mighty through God.

Anytime we want to talk about fighting the enemy, prayer is going to be on the list. The enemy will fight our prayer lives day and night. The enemy understands that prayer is communication with God. The enemy knows that God is a prayer-answering God, and the enemy does not want us to get a prayer through to the throne of God. I believe that we must be persistent in prayer. In the midst of being persistent, we must know that God heard us the first time we prayed.

If we want to battle debt, we need to pray before pulling out that credit card. If we want to battle debt, we must pray before we sign those car loan papers. If we want to battle debt, we must pray before signing that home loan. If we want to battle debt, we must pray and ask God to give us financial wisdom. The financial battle is not won at the bank or credit union. The financial battle is won in the prayer room.

I have been guilty of not spending enough time in the prayer room, but over the years, I have learned a few things. The more time we spend in the prayer room, the more battles we will win on the battlefield. When I say *win*, I mean stomp the devil under our feet. Make sure he understands that we will not be defeated. The God that we serve is all-powerful.

Fasting is another way to get the victory over distractions. Fasting moves the flesh out of the way so that we can draw closer to

God. As we draw closer to God, we will begin to see ourselves the way He see us. We will also begin to understand the gifts and talents He has given us. We will grow in our desire to give Him glory and honor with our gifts. As we draw close to God, He will begin to reveal more to us. As we understand more of the calling and the road ahead, we can be well prepared for what lies ahead. Fasting is not easy for the flesh, but fasting will help overcome distractions.

Another way to overcome distractions is to change the environment you are in. When the surrounding or conditions that we are in is not conducive to our assignment, it time for a change. Sometimes when I'm sitting in the living room and my wife comes in and turns on the TV, it is no big deal. I can tune it out and do what I need to do. There are other times, however, when the TV is a distraction. When it is a distraction, I have to go into another room. I have to change my environment.

For some, it may not be a matter of just moving to a different room. It may be necessary to change your address completely. It may not be where we live; it could be our job in certain cases. A person can make good money serving alcohol in a bar, but now that you are walking with Christ, you no longer want to serve alcohol. It's time to change your work environment. We can't allow our environment to distract us. God will show us how to change to the right environment.

Look over your life and see what is distracting you from your God-given assignment. Once you realize what your distractions are, ask God to give you direction on how to deal with your distraction. He will give you the direction and tools to overcome all distractions. No more distracted driving.

CHAPTER 7

Make a U-turn

Then we turned around and headed back across the wilderness toward the Red Sea, just as the LORD had instructed me, and we wandered around in the region of Mount Seir for a long time.

Then at last the LORD said to me, "You have been wandering around in this hill country long enough; turn to the north."

—Deuteronomy 2:1–3

There have been times when I was driving and would pass up the road I needed to turn on, or I would miss an exit off the freeway. When on the freeway, I simply go up and take the next exit. Then I get back on the freeway going in the opposite direction. Then when I get back to the exit I was supposed to take, I exited the freeway again. When driving on city streets or driving on a country road, if I pass where I want to go, I make a U-turn. A U-turn is turning a vehicle so that it is now moving in the opposite direction.

When I read the definition of *U-turn*, the first thing I thought about was repentance: turning away from the way we're walking and walking toward the Lord. A 180-degree turn. As we continue on this Christian journey that we are on, there will be many opportunities to repent or make a U-turn. I know that we should take advantage of every opportunity to repent. I can only speak for myself, but I make mistake after mistake and mistake. Which is a nice way of saying: I'm not perfect. I sin. Then I have to go back and get it right. Get things moving in the right direction again.

Sometimes we make small directional errors, and it is just a matter of making a quick U-turn and getting back on track. There are other times when the directional errors are more crucial. These errors can take longer to recover from to get back on track. The next exit might be a long way up the freeway, or it might just be too much traffic to make a quick U-turn. No matter how big or how small, the important thing is that we get back on the correct route. Getting back on the road to the right route will take us to where we want to be.

In our walk with Christ, there are times when we will make some bad decisions. There times when we will make an error in judgment. I think about court cases where a judge and jury will hear all the evidence and still end up sending an innocent person to jail or let a guilty person go free. It's not that they want to make the wrong decision; they are doing the best they can with the information that was presented. When we try to make decisions based on the info that was presented, we can make the same mistake.

When our relationship with God is good, and we are willing to walk in obedience, He can lead us down the right path consistently. However, there are times when sins enter and there is a separation between us and God. We have to go back and make a U-turn to restore the relationship and get back on track. Remember, God has not moved; we have move out of place because of our way of thinking. What do we do when our relationship with God is broken? First, we can take a look at some indications that there is a relationship issue.

When our relationship with God is not a priority, there is a relationship issue. Exodus 20:3 says, "You must not have any other god but me." As we go through life, many times we don't realize that we are putting things above God. There are times when I say to myself, *I will do my devotions after I finish watching this this TV show.* It may seem like a small thing, but if God has put it in my spirit to do devotions, I need to stop what I'm doing, get into a quiet place, and commune with God.

We can't even allow things that we think are spiritual to come between us and God. I can't say that I'm watching preaching on

YouTube so I don't need to read my Bible. If God tells me to read the Bible, that takes precedence over the YouTube preacher. I need to pause YouTube, pick up my Bible (or iPad nowadays), and read. The preacher may be anointed, but God can give more revelation than a preacher any day of the week.

What about that work that needs to be done down at the church? Too often, we let doing good work stop us from doing God's work. Yes, the work down at the church is important, and yes, the Lord knows that it needs to be done. The question is not how important the work is. The question is, what is the Lord leading you to do? Is the Lord saying, "Go down to the church and do the work," or is the Lord saying, "I want to spend quiet time with you right now"? There is someone the Lord is leading to do the work at the church. You need to be obedient to what the Lord is saying to you.

Our relationship with God must be the priority, not our relationship with the church, not our relationship with our pastor, not our relationship with our family, and not our relationship with each other. No relationship comes before our relationship with God. In all we do, we must keep our relationship with God as the priority.

We know that communication is a big deal in relationships. How is our communication with God? Even when it seems like God is not speaking, God is speaking. The communication issue is always on our end. We are too busy with life to get to a quiet place and hear what the Lord is saying for this season of our life. Are we not paying attention to understand that He is speaking?

I was driving one day on an interchange between two highways. A big rig started to come over, and I was able to slow down and get behind him. That was God speaking. God was saying, "I'm your protector. I give you traveling mercies." If we are not paying attention, we miss that. When a large expense comes out of nowhere, and the money is there to take care of it, that is God speaking. He is saying, "I'm Jehovah Jireh. I will supply all your needs." He is saying, "I'm your financial counselor." When you wake up each morning, that's God speaking. He is saying, "I protected you all night long. I watched you while you slumbered and slept." He is saying, "I woke you up at the appointed time. It's time to start your day in communion with Me."

When you open that refrigerator door and pick out anything you want to eat, that is God speaking. He is saying, "The same way I provide food for your physical body, I bless those who hunger and thirst after righteousness." Every time you open that door and walk into your home, that is God speaking. He is saying, "I'm your shelter. I'm your shelter in the time of a storm." God is speaking.

In order for there to be communication, there must be a giver and a receiver. God is speaking. Are we receiving what He is saying? We can't let there be a breakdown in our communication with God. We must be ready to receive what He is saying throughout each day. We must have an expectation that He is going to speak throughout each day.

Prayer is also communication. That means the conversation must go both ways. Maybe it starts out with us speaking and God listening, but there needs to be a time when God is speaking and we are listening. What He has to tell us is more important than what we have to tell Him. He already knows what we are going to say. We should go into prayer with great anticipation of what He is going to say to us.

Many times when it comes to communication, the issue is that we don't communicate at all. When we feel that things are going well, there is no time for God. It's only when we feel that we need something from Him that we have time to communicate. God is not seeking a superficial relationship with us. He is seeking a relationship that goes deeper. A relationship where we desire to commune with Him throughout the day every day. A desire to talk to Him and hear from Him.

A communication issue can be easily fixed. Just begin talking with God and begin to listen when He speaks. When the communication with God is right, there will be no need for U-turns. He will keep us on the right path. When it is time to turn, He will tell us to turn, and because we are listening for His voice, we will receive His directions and stay on the right path. We want a great communication with Jesus.

Another distraction that can happen in our relationship with God is routine. I'm not truly seeking a relationship with God. I'm not really trying to communicate with God. I'm just going through the motions. The preacher said I should pray each morning; therefore, I wake up each morning and pray. The preacher said I should pray each night before bed, so I pray each night before bed. I not truly trying to communicate with God. I'm just looking to check the box.

Our time with God shouldn't be a check-the-box exercise. A check-the-box exercise is when I'm doing something just so I can say I did it. Our time with God should come from a place of love: loving God and knowing that God loves us. Our time with God is not about checking the box. Our time with God is about building intimacy with Him; reading His Word to get to know Him better; desiring to see what His Word reveals about His character; spending time in prayer; seeking His face and a closer relationship. We should have a desire to spend time with Him, not feel forced to spend time with Him. Anytime we spend with God will not be in vain.

Another issue we may encounter in a relationship is taking the other person for granted. Taking someone for granted is when we do not properly appreciate the other person in the relationship. We can't see God, and that can make it easy to take Him for granted. We overlook all the things that He is doing in our lives, and we believe that we are making things happen. We should never underestimate the hand of God at work in our lives. Even when we can't see Him at work in our lives, He is working. Without God, we would surely fail.

That promotion did not come because we are so great. The promotion came because God moved on the heart of the person making the decision. I think of several promotions I have gotten where I was not the most qualified person. In one case, they offered the job to a couple of other people before me, but God moved them out of the way. How can I not acknowledge that God gave me the promotion? How can I not give God all the glory, honor, and praise that He is due?

When we take God for granted, it hurts the relationship. When we start to think we can do it on our own, we stop seeking to hear from God. That is when we get off track. When we start to think, *I don't see the hand of God; this was all me*, that is when we get off track. Being off track in our relationship or our purpose in God is not a good place to be. But we can rejoice; there is good news.

The good news is when we go to God and say, "I have tried it on my own long enough. I have made decisions without You long enough. I want You to take control." At that point, God will show us the U-turn. He will show how to get back on track with our purpose, with our destiny. He is such a loving and merciful God. He will not force us back to Him, but when we are ready, He will be waiting with open arms. If we have taken God for granted, it's time to make a U-turn and get back on track.

> If we claim we have no sin, we are only fooling ourselves and not living in the truth. But if we confess our sins to him, he is faithful and just to forgive us our sins and to cleanse us from all wickedness. (2 John 1:8–9)

Another issue we find in relationships is the failure to appreciate the other person. We diminish the value of the contribution that they make in our lives. You can see this with a husband that makes most of the money or a wife that makes most of the money. The spouse that is bringing in the most money can diminish the value of the other spouse. We never want to diminish the value of our significant other. We don't want to diminish the value of having God in our lives.

In Deuteronomy 2:1, Moses reminds the people of their journey. Due to disobedience, they couldn't enter the promised land. They would end up in the wilderness for the next forty years. For many, it will take a wilderness experience to bring us to a place where we trust God. When all the disobedient generation died, it was time to enter the promised land. There are some things in our lives that need to die. There are some things in our lives that will keep us from God's best. It's time to let some relationships die. It's time to let bad decisions die. Whatever needs to die, we need to let it die.

After all that generation died, Deuteronomy 1:2 says, "Then at last the LORD said to me…" The Lord will give you the direction you need when you are ready. After everything that needed to die has died, the Lord spoke. Deuteronomy 1:3 says, "You have been wandering around in this hill country long enough; turn to the north." It's time to make a U-turn. It's time to move in the direction that God has desired for us to go all along.

There must come a point in our lives when we get tired of wandering around in the wilderness. There must come a point where we get tired of going in circles. A time when we turn to the Lord and say, "I have tried it my way long enough. I need a U-turn experience. My way has not taken me anywhere. I need a U-turn experience. I have learned some things in this wilderness experience, and I know it is time to make a U-turn. Food and water were not readily available in the wilderness. I had to learn to trust You, God. I had to learn to trust You for food and water."

Deuteronomy 29:5 says, "And I have led you forty years in the wilderness: your clothes are not waxen old upon you, and thy shoe is not waxen old upon thy foot." There was no place to go in the wilderness to get the latest fashions. "I learned to trust You to put clothes on my back." There was not a shoe shop in the wilderness to get the latest shoes. "I had to trust You to keep shoes on my feet."

It is time to make a U-turn and get back on track to receive what God desires for us. God is not waiting for us to fail. He is leading us down a path to success. If any have wandered off the path, it is time to get back on the road of victory. Make a U-turn.

Hebrews 13:8 says, "Jesus Christ is the same yesterday, today, and forever." This tells me that the same God who was with the Children of Israel in the wilderness is the same God with us today. He has not changed and will not change. He will take care of us the same way He took care of them. When will we be ready to end our wilderness experience? When will we be ready to make a U-turn? The time is now.

CHAPTER 8

Slow Down Ahead

And we know that all things work together for good to them that
love God, to them who are the called according to his purpose.

—Romans 8:28

There are times when I get on the road and traffic is flowing
good. Then all of a sudden, the GPS will say there is a slowdown ahead. It serves as a warning to me. I need to get ready. I'm
going to have to slow down soon. The slowdown can be caused by a
variety of different issues. There can be road construction going on.
There can be an accident that is blocking one or more lanes, or a
stalled vehicle blocking a lane. Sometimes it is just lookie-loos. They
are trying to see something on the other side of the road, and that
causes the slowdown.

When you are on the road and are trying to get someplace
quick, needing to make a meeting or an appointment, a slowdown
can be frustrating. It will be easy to sit there upset at the situation. It
will be easy to jump to the negative and start complaining. Getting
upset, getting negative, or even starting to complain will not move
the traffic any quicker.

There are things that the enemy will bring against us to try and
slow us down in our calling. Getting upset, getting negative, or complaining will not help. In these times, all we can do is look to Jesus.

I'm learning to turn on worship music and just be patient as I sit in traffic. Spending that time with the Lord is a great benefit for me. Remember, the enemy can't bring it unless God allows it.

There are many things the enemy will throw at us to try and slow down our progress for the kingdom of God. The enemy does not want to see the kingdom of God advance at all. He will try to use potholes, traffic jams, accidents, and many other tactics to slow us down. He wants us to throw in the towel. He wants to stop or at least slow down our progress for the kingdom. The enemy's main goal is to stop ministry and to get as many souls in hell as he can.

One of the ways the enemy will stop or slow down ministry is with potholes. A pothole a depression or hollow in a road surface caused by wear or sinking. The enemy wants to cause spiritual potholes in our lives. When we get caught up in doing too many things, it can wear us down. Brotherhood chair, head of the deacon board, cleaning the church, taking care of the church grounds, working a full-time job, and having a family that needs you—this is a recipe for wear. This person will get worn out quickly.

Eventually the brotherhood will suffer when this person has worn down. The deacon board will suffer when this person has worn down. The family of this person will also feel the effects of him being worn down. It is okay to say no to the pastor and pray for God to send the right person. God knows the need of the ministry. We can't allow ourselves to become potholes that slow down the ministry.

Potholes are also formed by erosion. It may take some time for the ground underneath the road to erode enough to become a pothole, but if the erosion is not dealt with, it will happen. One of the ways erosion happens is listening to the wrong people. The wrong people could be family and friends who are not kingdom focused. The wrong people could be serving right alongside you in the ministry. When someone is not kingdom focused and they don't want you to be kingdom focused, don't spend time listening to that person. Don't get eroded and become a pothole.

If you live in the state of Washington and have to drive on I-5 in the afternoons, you will understand this next one. The enemy will try to use traffic jams to slow down the work of the kingdom.

A traffic jam is a long line of traffic at a standstill or moving slower than normal. There can be many causes of traffic jams. A couple of days ago, I was driving home from work. A couple of work trucks left what appeared to be a manhole cover on the roadway. Nobody wants to destroy their car. Drivers were slowing down and driving carefully over the manhole cover or moving into different lanes. This caused a disruption in traffic. It caused a traffic jam. It caused the drivers on the road to be delayed getting to their destination.

The enemy will try to throw all kinds of objects on the road ahead of us to slow us down. He is hoping we will get discouraged and give up, but the devil is a liar. We serve a God who can lead us around any obstacle in the road ahead. We just have to put our trust in Him.

The enemy will use car accidents to slow us down. An accident happens unexpectedly. One driver is driving to their destination, and another driver wants to change lanes. All of a sudden, you have two cars trying to occupy the same space. There is damage and injuries and sometimes death. It was unintentional, but it will have the effect of traffic. It will slow you down.

The enemy will also bring accusations to the people of God. It is not hard to do. The enemy will claim that the people of God have done something illegal or wrong. Negativity fills the news most days. To be honest, sometimes the accusations are true, but many times the accusations are false. The enemy wants to discredit our name. He wants us to have a bad reputation. In Acts 6, the lying witnesses said, "This man is always speaking against the holy temple and against the law of Moses. We have heard him say that this Jesus of Nazareth will destroy the temple and change the customs Moses handed down to us."

They gave false testimony to discredit Stephen. The same way the enemy did this in the early church, he is doing it today. Many times, it is Christian brothers and sisters trying to discredit one another. That is a sad thing. I know the devil rejoices when he sees brothers and sisters in Christ trying to discredit one another. We should never allow the devil to use us to tear down our brothers and sisters in Christ.

The enemy will use criticism to try and slow down or stop ministry from moving forward. There have been many times I stepped out of the pulpit to hear criticism. When constructive criticism is needed, we need to receive it and learn from it. When it is just downright good-for-nothing criticism, we have to learn how to move past it. If we are going to have success in ministry, we must be able to deal with criticism and move on.

Jesus had to deal with the critics of His day. No matter what He did, it seems like one group or another had something to say. How did Jesus handle the criticism? In 1 Peter 2:23, He did not retaliate when He was insulted, nor threatened revenge when He suffered. He left His case in the hands of God, who always judges fairly. We should always try to follow this example. Leave it in the hands of God. We can never go wrong when we put anything in the hands of God.

When dealing with criticism, we must follow the Word of God in James 1:19. Understand this, my dear brothers and sisters: You must all be quick to listen, slow to speak, and slow to get angry. There have been many times when I respectfully listened to something someone had to say. That does not mean I received it, but out of respect, I did listen. We never know when the right criticism will come, and we can make changes to move our ministry to a new level in God.

James 1:19 also tells us to be slow to become angry. There is a good reason God wants us to be slow to get angry. James 1:20 says human anger does not produce the righteousness God desires. When we operate out of anger, God does not get the glory, God does not get the honor, and God does not get the praise that He deserves. As we minster, we want God to be lifted up; therefore, we should not allow criticism to get us angry. We should seek to give God the glory in the midst of the criticism.

The higher we go, the greater the fight we will have. The ones who can take the criticism and keep going are the ones who will succeed. The ones who allow the criticism to beat them down will not succeed. They will be caught in the slowdown or stop of traffic. I believe that in God we can soar high above any criticism the enemy brings against us.

The enemy will use sickness and disease to slow down or stop ministry from going forward. This can be a tough one to overcome. When we are not feeling well in our bodies, it is difficult to teach, preach, or serve in any way. We find ourselves spending time in the emergency room instead of going to Sunday morning service, or heading to urgent care instead of heading to Bible study. My wife and I are constantly praying for good health. We constantly bind every spirit and infirmity and loose health and healing.

Not every sickness and disease is from the devil. When sickness and disease is from God, it is working for our good. God is wanting to put something in us, or He wants to take something from us. His purpose is to help us draw closer to Him. As we draw closer to Him, we can accomplish greater works. When sickness and disease is from the devil, he does not have our good in mind. He wants to shut us down.

When the enemy wants to shut us down with sickness and disease, we should remember what the Bible says in 1 Peter 2:24: "He personally carried our sins in his body on the cross so that we can be dead to sin and live for what is right. By his wounds you are healed." Whatever sickness and disease the enemy can bring, God can heal. Matthew 9:35 says, "Jesus traveled through all the towns and villages of that area, teaching in the synagogues and announcing the good news about the kingdom. And he healed every kind of disease and illness." This verse is clear on the matter. Not a few sicknesses and diseases, but every sickness and disease.

There are many sicknesses and diseases that doctors would say there is no cure for. They will say, "There is nothing we can do." They are right. With their limited ability, there is no cure. But the good news is that our God does not have the limitations of man. Our God is not limited to the medications in pills invented by man. Our God is not limited to what modern science has found. Our God is all-powerful. There is nothing too hard for God. He is Jehovah-Rapha, God our healer.

When God has given you an assignment, and the enemy wants to bring sickness and disease, get into your prayer closet. Let God know that you are ready to walk in your assignment, but you need

Him to step in and heal your body. If He does not give instant healing, He will give you the strength that you need as you go through the healing process. I will say this over and over: There is no God like our God. When the doctor says no, be ready for Jesus to say yes.

Another tool the enemy will use to try and slow down or stop the work of the kingdom is sinful pride. Proverbs 16:18 says, "Pride goes before destruction, and haughtiness before a fall." We don't want the sin of pride to come in and slow down the work of God. We have to be careful that when the Lord is blessing, we don't get caught up in pride. We must continually give Him the glory, the honor, and the praise.

Proverbs 11:2 says, "Pride leads to disgrace, but with humility comes wisdom." The Word of God does not lie. Pride will lead to disgrace, and it will slow down or stop the ministry that God wants to do in our lives. On the other hand, when we walk in humility, we understand that we can accomplish nothing without God. Instead of looking at success and seeing what we have done, we will look at success and see what the Lord has done. Every step we take in ministry is because the Lord allows us to take it. When our ministries go to the next level, it is the Lord's doing.

Proverbs 16:5 says, "The LORD detests the proud; they will surely be punished." This verse is letting us know that in the eyes of God, pride is a disgusting thing. Pride is wickedness in the eyes of God. How can God use us when we are doing something that is disgusting and wicked in His sight? If we want to be used by God, we cannot allow the enemy to put pride in our heart. Don't get caught up in the deception of pride.

James 4:6 says, "And he gives grace generously." As the scriptures say, "God opposes the proud but gives grace to the humble." We must choose humility over pride. If God is for us, He is more than the whole world against, but if God opposes us, what can the world do to help? To oppose is to work against or resist. We should choose the humble road and not be opposed to God.

The enemy will also use persecution to stop or slow down the work that we are assigned to do for the kingdom of God. The enemy will continuously come against our Christian beliefs. Galatians 4:29

says, "But you are now being persecuted by those who want you to keep the law, just as Ishmael, the child born by human effort, persecuted Isaac, the child born by the power of the Spirit." The flesh wants to persecute the spirit.

When you hear the world say that trusting in God is a sign of weakness, or Christians say they trust in God because they don't want to take responsibility for their actions, that is the enemy persecuting the church. The enemy would love for us to think that, because of the persecution, trusting in God is a sign of weakness. Then he can get us on the road to trusting ourselves.

The enemy wants us to believe that trusting God is a way not to take responsibility for our actions. The truth of the matter is this: the responsible thing to do is trust God and put our lives in His hands. Romans 14:12 says, "Yes, each of us will give a personal account to God. In the end we all must be accountable to God for the choices we made in this life."

The enemy will try to bring slowdowns ahead into our ministry as much as he can. What we must do is trust God to get us around the slowdown or to take us through the slowdown. Don't allow the slowdown to become a stop. Keep moving from faith to faith and from glory to glory. Keep going, and let God get all the glory.

Isaiah 43:18–19 says, "But forget all that. It is nothing compared to what I am going to do. For I am about to do something new. See, I have already begun! Do you not see it? I will make a pathway through the wilderness. I will create rivers in the dry wasteland." Even in a slowdown, don't give up. Watch God do a new thing. If He can make a path in the wilderness, He can make a new path for me and you to get around the slowdown. He will show the way to get around all the tricks of the adversary. Slowdown ahead? That's okay. Keep moving forward in God.

CHAPTER 9

You Are Back Online

Remain in me, and I will remain in you. For a branch
cannot produce fruit if it is severed from the vine, and
you cannot be fruitful unless you remain in me.
Yes, I am the vine; you are the branches. Those who
remain in me, and I in them, will produce much
fruit. For apart from me you can do nothing.

—John 15:4–5

There are times in my life when I will be surfing the Internet
looking for information, or at work trying to get what I need
for an assignment. I click the link to go where I need to go, and all
of a sudden, I get a message that says, "It looks like you are offline."
It is telling me that there is no connection between my computer or
device and the Internet. There is no communication between the
two. The online symbol goes away, and another symbol takes its
place to tell me "Not connected to Wi-Fi."

There are times when I'm driving in my car and the GPS will
lose its connection. This usually happens when I'm driving in an area
with a lot of trees or I'm driving in the mountains. The trees and the
mountains tend to block the signal. After a while, you will hear the
phone say you are back online. It is letting me know that I'm connected again and getting good direction again.

John 15:4–5 lets us know that if we do not stay connected to God, we can do nothing, and we will be fruitless. All that we want to accomplish in the world for the kingdom depends on us staying connected to God. The enemy comes to steal, kill, and destroy. One of the main things the enemy wants to destroy is our connection with God. If he can destroy our connection, he can stop our work for God.

The enemy will try to break our connection with God by putting barriers or obstructions between us and God. A barrier is designed to prevent access to something or someone. One barrier is comfort. I'm comfortable in this place; why would I want to move to another place? My ministry is going well; why would I want to change anything? Business has never been better; why would I change anything?

Being comfortable at our current level of ministry or success will create an environment where we will not be seeking to hear from God and are willing to let the connection die. We have no desire to hear God tell us to move out of our comfort zone. When we are in our comfort zone, we don't believe that there is any need to rock the boat. We don't believe that there is any need to do anything different or improve on the status quo.

Interference from other sources is a big issue. I have a couple of GPS apps on my phone. When I get into my car, there is one that I like to use. When I'm already driving and I need to ask the phone for directions, it uses the other app. One day, I was driving, and I set the address to where I wanted to go. However, at some point during the trip I realized that I needed to go to another place. I asked to phone to get directions to the other place. The phone got the directions and started telling them to me. The problem is that I still have the directions from the other app going and was getting two different directions. I was confused. What is going on? Why am I getting two different sets of directions?

It took some time, but once I realized that I had the other app still running, the solution was easy. I had to turn off the directions that were trying to take me home. Then when there was only one set of directions speaking, it was clear which way to go. If the Holy Spirit was the only voice speaking to us, it would be clear which way to go, but we have many voices trying to lead us in different directions. The more we spend time with God, the more we will know His voice when He speaks. Remember John 15:5: "Those who remain in me, and I in them, will produce much fruit." We want to produce much fruit for the kingdom of God.

Equipment failure is another issue with connectivity. In this case, I'm talking about the equipment known as the heart of man. Throughout the world, we see more and more that the heart of man does not have a desire to be connected and operating with God. When a heart does not want to be connected with God, there is an equipment failure. When the heart toward God is failing, we need to fix it and fast.

People refuse to come to God or they turn away from God for many reasons. One is that the desires of the flesh don't line up with biblical teaching. Another reason could be that they are searching through many different religions, and they find something in another religion that they like more. It could be that they want to fit in will all their Christian friends. Whatever the reason might be, a heart that does not want to be connected with God needs to be fixed. There is an equipment issue.

Many church youth programs today are more interested in the kids having fun than they are in teaching biblical truths. There are five hundred kids in our youth program. This is good to hear, but how many of those kids maintain a relationship with Christ after the age of eighteen? That is the sign of success in a youth program. Are we teaching kids how to have a connection with God? Are we teaching kids about relationship with God? School gets them eight hours a day; social media gets them all day. The church gets forty-five minutes to an hour a week. How impactful do we want that time to be?

It is time to renew our connection with God. It is time that you are back online. Being online simply means you are connected. We must be online with God. We must be connected to God. When our connection with God is broken, we need to find the problem and the fix. One of the ways we can fix a broken connection with God is to reboot.

Booting a computer is starting the system software on the computer. The term *reboot* simply means to start the computer software again. This needs to be done when there is an issue with the software. In our walk with Christ, it is not just about starting again. We need to get rid of some bad teaching. We need to get rid of some unhealthy relationships. We need to get rid of some bad habits. The good news is we don't have to do these things on our own. God will help us get rid of the bad habits. God will help us get out of unhealthy relationships. God will help us delete poor teaching. God will help us get connected again.

We need to keep our antivirus software up to date. The enemy tries to trick us in three ways: the lust of the eyes, the lust of the flesh, and the pride of life. He does not make it obvious to us; he tries to disguise his tricks so we don't see them coming. That is why we must keep our antivirus software up to date. How do we keep our antivirus up to date? Romans 12:1–2 says we must allow the Holy Spirit to renew our minds daily. First Peter 5:8 says, "Stay alert and be watchful." When our mind is renewed, we are alert and watchful. There is not a devil in hell that can turn off our connection with God.

The more our mind is renewed, the stronger the connection will be. The more we allow God to renew our mind, the more we will seek connectivity with Him. A renewed mind understands that the enemy is on the prowl. A renewed mind understands that the enemy wants to take us out. A renewed mind will stay alert, and a renewed mind will be watchful. If we allow ourselves to be conformed to this world, we will be easy prey for the devil. He will have no problem breaking our connection to God.

Conforming to the world is to assimilate to the values of this world. Instead of holding to the values of Christ, we begin to hold to the values of this world. That is a road we don't want to go down. Usually, it is not overnight. The enemy keeps it going little by little, day by day. Today you are willing to compromise here. Tomorrow, you are willing to compromise there. One day, you look up and find you are conformed to the world's values and lifestyle.

We have the television, radio, Internet, family, friends, and coworkers downloading into us each day. The question is, how much bandwidth do we give God to download into us? How many megabytes per second do we give God? When it is time to sit quietly with God, how focused are we on Him? When it is time to spend quiet time with God, how focused are we on all the other things going on in our lives?

Bandwidth deals with the amount of data transmitted in a certain amount of time. If I'm giving God one hour a day, will I give Him all my bandwidth for that hour? I have often heard it said that it is not the quantity but the quality of time. Are we spending quality time with God each day? Does He have our undivided attention to download all that we need? Is He sharing the bandwidth available with something else?

Give God the bandwidth that is necessary for Him to give you what He desires to download into you each day of your life. Give God the bandwidth that He needs to give you the directions that you need to take your ministry to the next level. Give God the bandwidth that is necessary for Him to give you directions for your marriage. The list can keep going. The main point is to let God download into you daily. Give Him the bandwidth.

I work with the maintenance team at my job. We get calls that say a machine is down or not running properly. When that call comes, the job of the team is to go out and troubleshoot the issue. Sometimes it is something simple that can be fixed in a few minutes. Other times, the issue is more complex and requires more time to troubleshoot or fix. Machines can be down for hours, days, weeks, months, and, yes, even years. Sometimes it is a matter of whether the machine is important enough to pay the price to fix it.

If a team came out to us today and did some troubleshooting on our connection to the Holy Spirit, what would they find? Would they find a connection that is working at peak capacity? Would they find a connection issue that is a quick fix? Would they find a connection that will take months or even years to fix?

We should all do some troubleshooting on our connection line to the Holy Spirit. Test it out to see if all is working correctly. Is communication going back and forth the way it should? If we find that there are some issues along the way, will we consider it important enough to fix it? If it is not important enough to fix, what do we think we can replace it with? What can replace the connection to the Holy Spirt in our lives? The answer is plain and simple: nothing. Our connection to the Holy Spirit must be maintained.

There are times when the team goes out to a machine and find that it is just a settings issue. Someone has changed the settings to something that will not work. I should say the settings will work but will not produce well. There are times in our lives when we need to look at our settings. This once again goes back to the mind. Has something caused a reset in our mind?

Philippians 2:5 says, "You must have the same attitude that Christ Jesus had." The KVJ says, "Let this mind be in you, which was also in Christ Jesus." As Christians, our minds should be on a setting that has us desiring the things of Christ. Christ walked in compassion. We should have a mindset of compassion. Christ walked in humility. We should have a mindset of humility. Christ walked in self-sacrifice. We should have a mindset of self-sacrifice. Christ walked in servanthood. We should have a mindset of servanthood.

If the person next to you could see your mindset, would they see a mindset that reflects the mindset of Jesus Christ? Ephesians 4:23 reads, "And be renewed in the spirit of your mind." As we walk with Christ, we should be putting away the old self more and more. Each day, we should be made new in the spirit of our minds. Each day, we should strive for a deeper connection with the Holy Spirit.

To improve our connection with the Holy Spirit, we need to make sure we have an updated router. The router is the device that sends information to the device that we are using. We need to make sure we are getting information from reliable sources. We can't listen to every preacher who has a YouTube channel. We can't trust every Facebook page and Twitter (or X) feed. Not every book that comes out has accurate information.

The sources we use should be God-centered and not self-centered. A God-centered resource will keep God in focus. A God-centered resource will teach dependence on God and tell us to lean on God. A God-centered resource will lead us to trust in God. A self-centered resource will talk about trusting yourself. We want to be God-centered at all times.

When listing to different preachers, make sure they are giving the Bible book, chapter, and verse. Don't be afraid to study for yourself. Research what the preacher said to make sure the information was correct. Many of these little sound bites sound good. It is not just about the information sounding good; the information needs to be good. The information needs to line up with the Word of God. If it does not line up with the Word of God, throw it out of your mind. Make sure you are getting good information from your sources.

John 15:4 says, "Remain in me, and I will remain in you. For a branch cannot produce fruit if it is severed from the vine, and you cannot be fruitful unless you remain in me." Jesus is talking about staying connected in this verse. To remain in God, we must stay connected to God, knowing that He will supply all that we need. All that we try to do will come to nothing if we are not connected to Jesus. That is why the connection is so important. We cannot allow the connection to fail.

John 15:5 says, "Yes, I am the vine; you are the branches. Those who remain in me, and I in them, will produce much fruit. For apart from me you can do nothing." In this verse, He is letting us know that He is the source that supplies our needs. Branches that are cut off from the vine will die. Branches that remain connected to the vine will receive all that they need to live and thrive.

Being offline is one of the worst places a Christian can be. When we are in a place we can't hear from God or don't want to hear from God, it's time for a shift. We should always be intentional about our relationship with God, but when we go offline, we must be intentional about getting back online with our Savior. He will never leave us alone.

I pray that anyone who has lost their connection to God will get back online. Anyone who is on the verge of backsliding will get back online. The connection to God is the most important connection in your life. All you have to do is ask. When you ask God for a reconnection, you will hear the words, "You are back online."

CHAPTER 10

Detour Ahead

But the centurion, willing to save Paul, kept them from
their purpose; and commanded that they which could swim
should cast themselves first into the sea, and get to land:
And the rest, some on boards, and some on broken pieces of the
ship. And so it came to pass, that they escaped all safe to land.

—Acts 27:43–44

There are times when on the road trying to get someplace, you come
across a sign that says "Detour Ahead." Traffic on the detour is
usually a lot slower, and it takes you longer to get where you are going.
There are times when a professional player has plans for his or her career,
but suddenly, they have an injury. The injury makes them change their
plans. You can say their career took a detour. Even in business, a person
can have plans for where they want their business to go and how they
want it to get there. Something causes a change in the economy, and the
business stalls for a while. That business just had a detour.

A detour can be defined in a few different ways. Taking a round-
about to avoid something like road construction is a detour. Taking
the long way around so that you can visit or see something out the
way is also a detour. Any deviation from the normal or direct route
is a detour. Going in a direction that is not planned or expected is
called a detour.

In some cases, the detour is planned. You know it is going to take longer. You know it is out of the way, but you don't mind. There is something or someone you want to see, or there is someplace you want to go. When a detour is planned, it's not so bad, I would assume. When a detour is not planned, it can get frustrating. There was no time to plan for the detour, but it is here now, and you must deal with it. The way you planned to go is not available to you anymore. There is a detour that will allow you to get to your destination.

There are many examples in the Bible of God taking people on a detour. Job and his wife were taken on a great detour. One day, all was going well for Job and his wife. The next day, Job and his wife were on a detour. A detour they had not planned to be on. A detour that they did not see coming. The Sabean raiders stole all their animals and killed all the farmhands they had, except one. Fire from heaven came down and burned up all their sheep and killed all the shepherds they had, except one. The Chaldean raiders stole all their camels and killed all the servants they had, except one. A powerful wind caused the house their kids were in to collapse. All seven of their sons and all three of their daughters died. They lost all ten of their children in one day.

Moses was born at a time when all newborn Hebrew males were to be thrown into the Nile River. We come to the first detour for Moses. He was not thrown into the Nile River. He was hidden by his mother. When she could no longer hide him, she put him in a waterproof basket and put it in the river. Instead of being eaten by the alligators in the Nile, Moses is found by Pharaoh's daughter and raised in Pharaoh's home.

One day, after Moses had grown up, he went to visit his people. He killed one of the Egyptians. His life took a detour. Now he had to leave the luxury of the palace and go on the run. God brought him to the land of Midian and gave him a wife there. I'm sure Moses thought he would live out the rest of his days in Midian. However, God had another detour for Moses. God told Moses to go back to Egypt. God wanted to use Moses to deliver His people from bondage.

Joshua's life had a detour. Instead of just fighting to take his part of the land, he is given the responsibility of leading all the Children of Israel into the promised land. Samson's life took a detour because he played with his gift. Samson was strong and could take out the Philistines who came against him. One day, he revealed the secret of his strength to Delilah. Then his life took a detour. They cut his hair and gouged out his eyes. God still used him one last time to kill more Philistines at his death then he had killed in his entire life.

Gideon had a detour in his life. Gideon was just threshing wheat at the bottom of a winepress. He was trying to hide the grain from the Midianites. The Midianites were used by God to punish the Children of Israel because they chose to worship other gods. The Midianites treated the Children of Israel so harshly that they cried out to the Lord. This sounds like my life sometimes. When all is going well, I just go about by business like I have it all under control. Then when tough times come, I cry out to the Lord.

God is a merciful God. He hears me when I call to Him every time. He heard the Children of Israel cry out to Him. That was when Gideon had a detour in his life. God sent an angel to talk with Gideon. Gideon told the angel, "We have heard about the miracles of the Lord from our ancestors, but we are oppressed. We have heard about the deliverance of our ancestors, but we are oppressed." Gideon told the angel, "The Lord has abandoned us."

It is amazing how we can walk away from God and do everything He tells us not to do. As soon as something goes wrong, we feel like God has abandoned us. God has not abandoned us. He is putting our life on a detour so that He can bring us back into relationship with Him. He is allowing us to go on a detour so we can see that we need Him. We should thank God for the detours of life.

Gideon went from threshing wheat to being told to go and deliver Israel from the Midianites. This detour was not just about Gideon. This detour was for a nation. Gideon doubted for a while but eventually accepted the detour. Gideon started out with an army of thirty-two thousand. Then a detour happened, and twenty-two thousand went back home. God was not finished yet. God allowed another detour, and Gideon was left with three hundred men to go to war. God fought the battle for them, and the three hundred men defeated the army of the Midianites. You can read about Gideon in Judges chapters 6 and 7.

The apostle Paul had a different life before his detour. Paul, known as Saul, was a devout Jew, a Pharisee, and a persecutor of Christians. In Acts 9, we read that Saul was uttering threats and was eager to kill the Christians. He requested a letter from the high priest to take to the synagogues in Damascus. He wanted their cooperation in arresting the followers of Christ. Saul was on a mission.

However, when Saul was on the way to Damascus, he came to a detour. The detour came in the form of a light from heaven. It caused Saul to fall to the ground. God asked Saul a question. The question was simple: "Saul! Saul! Why are you persecuting Me?" Saul then had to ask this question: "Who are You, Lord?" Jesus answered by saying, "I am Jesus, the one you are persecuting! Now get up and go into the city, and you will be told what you must do."

Paul's entire purpose was changed when he came to his detour. No more killing Christians; now Saul was directed to pray for them. No more having Christians arrested but being used by God to cause people to become Christians. Without the detour of Paul, there would be no book of Romans, Galatians, Philippians, and so on. Saul's detour, by the grace of God, is still changing lives today.

King David had a life that had some detours. He was just a little shepherd boy watching over his father's sheep. He would kill the animals that came in to kill the sheep. That is written in 1 Samuel 13:34–37. When Samuel came to anoint the next king of Israel, David's father did not think enough of David to call him in. There are doubters all around us, but when God gets ready to promote His people, the promotion comes despite man.

David thought it was going to be just another day watching the sheep. Then the detour happened. David was called in. When he was called in, Samuel anointed him to be the king of Israel. First Samuel 16:13 says, "So as David stood there among his brothers, Samuel took the flask of olive oil he had brought and anointed David with the oil. And the Spirit of the LORD came powerfully upon David from that day on. Then Samuel returned to Ramah."

David had another detour in his life. Jesse, David's father, sent him to take some supplies to his brothers who were in King Saul's camp. All David must do is take his brothers the supplies, see how they are doing, and go back home. That sounds easy to me, but it's detour time. A giant named Goliath speaks out while David is there. Remember 1 Samuel 16:13: the Spirit of the Lord was powerfully upon David. David knew that the champion of the Philistines was no match for the Champion of Israel. The Champion of Israel is the Lord God Almighty. David defeated the giant by the grace of God. A detour saved Israel.

Mary and Joseph had a detour. They had everything planned out. "We will be betrothed for the allotted amount of time. When the time comes, we will get married. We will not be together sexually until after we are married." Sounds good. Sounds like the godly way of doing things. God sent an angel to Mary. The angel told her that she would become pregnant by the Holy Spirit. What a detour. This detour was so radical that God had to send an angel to Joseph to confirm the story that Mary had told him. They both accepted this radical detour, and the King of kings and the Lord of lords was born over two thousand years ago.

In Judges 4, we find Deborah. Deborah was the wife of Lapidoth. She was also judging Israel. She is doing what God called her to do, sitting under her palm tree. The Children of Israel came to her for judgment. Once again, Israel was doing evil in the sight of the Lord. The Lord turned them over to Jabin, the Canaanite king. They were ruthlessly oppressed for twenty years. Then they cried out to the Lord. Deborah called for Barak, son of Abinoam. The Lord wanted Barak to go and gather ten thousand warriors and go to battle against Sisera. Sisera was the commander of Jabin's army. The Lord had already given Barak and his warriors victory. Then the detour happened. Barak said to Deborah, "I will not go unless you go with me."

Instead of sitting under her palm tree judging the Children of Israel, Deborah was on her way to the battle. Sisera came to the battle with nine hundred iron chariots. When Barak led the warriors in battle, the Lord threw the warriors and chariots of Sisera into a panic.

Sisera escaped on foot, but all the other warriors were killed. Sisera was also killed by Jael, the wife of Heber. Israel became stronger and stronger against Jabin, the Canaanite king, until they finally defeated him.

In Joshua 2, we meet Rahab. Rahab was a woman who lived in Jericho. Rahab was a harlot. Joshua sent two spies to Jericho, and the king of Jericho was looking for them. Most people in Rahab's position would have turned the spies over to the king without even thinking about it. However, Rahab took a detour. She hid the spies from the king, and later that night, she helped them escape.

Before Rahab helped the spies escape, she made them promise to spare the lives of herself, her mother and father, her sister and brother, and their families. The spies promised to save their lives. When it came time to take the city, all of Rahab's family was saved. Rahab took a detour that saved many lives.

In Acts 27, Paul has another detour as a prisoner. He was on a ship headed to Italy. They ran into a tempestuous wind. They ran the ship aground and wanted to kill Paul and the other prisoners to keep them from escaping. Acts 27:43 says, "But the centurion, willing to save Paul, kept them from their purpose; and commanded that they which could swim should cast themselves first into the sea, and get to land." The Lord had a purpose for this detour. It was not time for Paul to die. There was still ministry that he had to do.

Verse 44 says, "And the rest, some on boards, and some on broken pieces of the ship. And so it came to pass, that they escaped all safe to land." They made it to the island of Melita. They were there for three months. Paul, by the grace of God, was able to heal those brought to him who were sick.

None of the detours in our life take God by surprise. I can tell you I have had to take many detours that I was not ready for, but God was ready for them all. God brought me out to Bremerton and saved me. I thought I would be at the ministry for the rest of my life—but detour. God called me to another ministry. I thought I would be a deacon in the church just like my daddy—but detour. God called me to the ministry. I thought I would only be at my job for a few years, and then something closer to home would come—but detour. I have been at my job for over twenty-six years.

God is truly showing me through the detours in my life that He is in control. That is true in all of our lives. God is in control. I have a plan for how I think my life will go in the next few years, but I'm learning a detour could be anywhere along the journey. God has a purpose for the detours He allows in our lives.

All the detours that happened in Moses's life was to get him to the place where God could use him to deliver the Children of Israel from Egypt. The last detour in his life where he was not able to enter the promised land is an example to us that there are consequences for sin. When I look at the detours in Samson's life, the first thing I learn is: don't play with the enemy. Samson could have accomplished more with his life had he not played with the enemy. The next thing I learn from Samson is to use gifts to bring God glory, not prove how great we are.

Job's detour is a little more difficult for me to understand. I can understand a little suffering here and a little suffering there to keep Job humble. That is not what God did. God allowed the enemy to take almost everything from Job, including his health and strength. Through Job, we see a man who can trust God with much but can also trust God with little. Job 13:15 says, "Though he slay me, yet will I trust in him: but I will maintain mine own ways before him." We also see that God can restore anything the enemy takes from us.

We should embrace the detour that God put in our lives. We should be thankful for every detour we have gone through and every detour you will ever go through. God is an intentional God. Everything that He does has a purpose. Every circumstance and situation that God allows to come our way has a purpose. I appreciate the detours of my life. Without them, I would not be the man I am today. I would not be where God wants me to be.

CHAPTER 11

Roadside Assistance

Ask, and it shall be given you; seek, and ye shall
find; knock, and it shall be opened unto you.

—Matthew 7:7

Each year close to seventy million drivers have some sort of issue with their car while they are on the road. Some can deal with the issue on their own, especially when it is a minor issue. Most drivers, however, will need to call for roadside assistance. I would guess that most insurance companies nowadays have a roadside assistance program. At least the insurance company that my wife and I use has it.

Roadside assistance in the normal world is limited. They provide services like changing flat tires, jump-starting a dead battery, delivering fuel when you have an empty fuel tank, and unlocking doors when you lock yourself out of the car. When they can't help you on the roadside, they will tow your vehicle to a place that can assist you. We can say that roadside assistance fixes what they can so you can continue driving. Towing services take your car to a place that can fix what can't be fixed on the roadside.

Roadside assistance was first offered in 1915. Today, roadside assistance plans give you one number to call wherever you need help, twenty-four hours a day, seven days a week. However, the times you can use it each year is limited, four service calls per year in some cases. Getting stuck on the side of the road isn't fun. When you're stranded, it is comforting to know that there is someone you can call.

When we look at the natural or physical roadside assistance, we can see that there is a great benefit to having it. In the spirit, we have a God who is roadside assistance for every area of our lives. There is no issue that we come across in our lives that the Holy Spirit cannot help us fix. Isaiah 9:6 says, "For unto us a child is born, unto us a son is given: and the government shall be upon his shoulder: and his name shall be called Wonderful, Counsellor, the mighty God, the everlasting Father, the Prince of Peace."

As we move along the road to our destiny in Christ, there will be many times we will need roadside assistance. We have a Counselor who meets us where we are. His office hours are twenty-four hours a day, and His phone line is never busy. Second Peter 3:9 says, "The Lord isn't really being slow about his promise, as some people think. No, he is being patient for your sake. He does not want anyone to be destroyed but wants everyone to repent." The Lord is waiting for us to come to Him. He will assist us in every area that the enemy wants to fight us in along the way.

The Holy Spirit is roadside assistance for marriage. The enemy will attack your marriage as you try to move forward on this Christian journey. I have seen different statistics for Christian marriages. Some sources say about 50 percent of Christian marriages end in divorce. Another resource says 20 to 25 percent. The truth is that no Christian needs to end in divorce. Take your marriage to God.

Genesis 2:24 says, "This explains why a man leaves his father and mother and is joined to his wife, and the two are united into one." The Holy Spirit will show a husband how to cleave to his wife. A man should love, honor, and cherish his wife. The leading of the Holy Spirit will show a man how to treat his wife. Proverbs 18:22 says, "The man who finds a wife finds a treasure, and he receives favor from the LORD." Men, when the enemy is fighting our marriages, let's not give in, but let's treat our wives like they are a treasure from God.

Proverbs 31:10 says, "Who can find a virtuous and capable wife? She is more precious than rubies." The enemy does not just fight husbands; he fights wives also. Anything he can do to take our minds off our ministries. Wives, when the enemy brings the fight, just let him know that you are more precious than rubies, and that you are going to act like the precious ruby you are. When the husband and the wife are acting like the Holy Spirit is leading them to act, the enemy will not be able to use your marriage in the fight.

The enemy will try to use your church in the fight against your ministry.

Even in the process of raising children, the Holy Spirit is our roadside assistance. Ephesians 6:4 says, "Fathers, do not provoke your children to anger by the way you treat them. Rather, bring them up with the discipline and instruction that comes from the Lord." Raising kids in any age and time could not have been easy, but I believe it is a lot tougher to raise kids today than it was a hundred years ago. In many cases, due to social media, kids know more about what is going on in the world than their parents.

Despite all that, the Holy Spirit can still give instructions on how to deal with your children today. The Holy Spirit knows more about our children than we ever could. Let the Holy Spirit lead in the child-rearing process, and we will see greater results. As parents, we do what we think is best or we do what our parents did. Neither way is right. Before God formed your child in the womb, He ordained them with purpose. Seek the Lord in prayer, and He will direct you in raising your child.

The enemy will use our finances to stop us from reaching our destiny. However, when our finances let us down along the way, we have financial roadside assistance. It is no secret that ministry takes money. Psalm 24:1 says, "The earth is the LORD's, and everything in it. The world and all its people belong to him." The Lord knows where all the money is all over the earth. He will supply the needs of your ministry. Don't let finances stop you. Call for roadside assistance, and God will show you the way.

Physical health is another area that the enemy will use to fight us. Tired, sick bodies don't help us minister the way we need to. Psalms 139:14 says, "Thank you for making me so wonderfully complex! Your workmanship is marvelous—how well I know it." First

Corinthians 3:16 says, "Don't you realize that all of you together are the temple of God and that the Spirit of God lives in you?" God made us, and He dwells in us. He wants us to be healthy. The little voice says no to the doughnuts, ice cream, and french fries. That's God. All we have to do is listen.

There are some physical health issues that require more than simple roadside assistance. When dealing with the more serious health issues, we can still put our trust in God. He will send complete healing, so that we can go do the work He has called us to do, or He will give us wisdom to work with the issue at hand. I have seen people with physical issues do wonderful things. Let God lead you and guide you on your physical health journey.

Many churches have closed their doors due to the failing mental health of the pastor. Many of our spiritual leaders are fighting depression and mental fatigue. The truth is it doesn't have to be this way. Mental health includes our emotional health and our psychological health. Our social well-being also comes into play when dealing with mental health. The state of our mental health plays a role in how we think, feel, and act. The way in which we handle stress, relate to others, and make healthy choices are all a part of our mental health.

The enemy can certainly attack our mental health if he wants to stop us. Psalms 42:11 says, "Why am I discouraged? Why is my heart so sad? I will put my hope in God! I will praise him again—my Savior and my God!" We should always hope in God. There may be times when we will need to see a mental health professional. There is no shame in that. God has given them to us with purpose. There are times when roadside assistance will not be enough. Seek the level of help that you need. Trust God during the process.

Emotional health is a part of our overall mental health. Emotional health is all about what we think and what we feel. Are my thoughts about helping someone or hurting someone? This is a sign of my emotional health. If I'm thinking about hurting someone, my emotional health is not good. When I'm willing to help others and do good, then I'm operating in good emotional health. Although we can't operate out of our emotions when doing the work of the kingdom, we need to have good emotional health.

I was watching a television show not too long ago. There was a lady doing a great job babysitting for people who needed it. On the surface, it seemed like this lady had good emotional health. She was only doing a good job to get recommendations so she could get a job babysitting an infant girl. Once she got a job babysitting a little girl, she kidnapped the little girl and attempted to kill her. There was something wrong with her emotional health.

Galatians 5:22–23 says, "But the Holy Spirit produces this kind of fruit in our lives: love, joy, peace, patience, kindness, goodness, faithfulness, gentleness, and self-control. There is no law against these things!" When we are operating in the fruits of the Holy Spirit, we are operating in sound emotional health. Not one of these nine fruits involves doing harm to anyone in any way.

The enemy will come against your emotional health. If he can't stop you one way, he will continue to try different ways. The important thing is to be aware of what you are thinking. If your thoughts don't line up with the Word of God, seek roadside assistance.

When doing the work of the kingdom, we will need to have good spiritual health. Spiritual heath has to do with our connection or relationship with God. When our connection is good with God, and we have good communion and our fellowship is good, we have good spiritual health.

Two of the ways the enemy will attack our spiritual health is to try and make us think that God is not real, or to get us to think that that God doesn't care about us. If the enemy can get us to believe that God is not real, we will stop seeking a relationship with Him. If we are not seeking a relationship with God, we have a problem. We also have a problem if we believe that God does not care about us. How can we take our problem to someone who does not care about us? Whenever we are not seeking God or are not in communion with God, it affects our spiritual health.

Psalms 116:12–14 says, "What can I offer the LORD for all he has done for me? I will lift up the cup of salvation and praise the LORD's name for saving me. I will keep my promises to the LORD in the presence of all his people." When the enemy wants us to think God is not real, all we have to do is look back over our lives. When the enemy wants us to think we don't need a relationship with God, all we have to do is look back over our lives. When we see all that we have come through, we will understand that there must be a God.

In order to stay in good spiritual health, we need to stay in prayer, and stay in the Word of God, stay in fellowship with God and other Christians. We must keep our mind fixed upon Him. Isaiah 26:3 says, "You will keep in perfect peace all who trust in you, all whose thoughts are fixed on you!" When our communion with God is strong, the enemy has no avenue to come in and affect our spiritual health.

Make a bad decision or two, and the enemy will surely come in and try to make you doubt every decision. You can make a hundred good decisions and one bad decision. Whenever it is time to make another decision, the enemy will bring that bad decision back to your memory. The enemy wants to make you doubt that you can make a good decision. The truth is we should not be making decisions on our own. Proverbs 28:26 says, "Those who trust their own insight are foolish, but anyone who walks in wisdom is safe."

Proverbs 3:6 says, "Seek his will in all you do, and he will show you which path to take." We should be seeking God when making decisions for kingdom business. We should be seeking God for decisions that we make in every area our lives. When God is directing our path, we will always be on the right path. Trust the Lord in your decision-making process.

There are so many other areas that we could discuss. However, I think we can see that whatever the problem is, God can fix it. Whatever the situation is, God is in control. God is just waiting on us to make the call. To give him an invitation to come in and assist. Too often, we think we have all the answers.

As long as we are on the road to our destiny, the enemy will try to get us to pull over and stop progressing, but the Lord God Almighty has roadside assistance available to get us back on the road again. With the Lord on our side, we can continue to advance the kingdom. We can continue working our God-given assignment as long as we keep our hand in His hand. Jeremiah 33:3 says, "Ask me and I will tell you remarkable secrets you do not know about things to come." Go to God in prayer with any issue that threatens to stop your progress. In the natural world, we would get our phone and make a call or go to an app. A dispatcher will send someone your way. In the Spirit, we call on God in prayer. He will dispatch His delivering angels.

The thing we need to remember about roadside assistance is that you have to ask. Matthew 7:7 says, "Ask, and it shall be given you; seek, and ye shall find; knock, and it shall be opened unto you: when we go to God in prayer he will answer." He will give us the answer that we need. God is the best roadside assistance anyone could ask for. In fact, He is better than roadside assistance.

When you call for roadside assistance, you are usually waiting anywhere from a half hour to an hour and a half. However, God does not have to travel for miles to get to where you are. He is right there beside you. God does not have to finish another call before He can get to your call. God does not have to answer calls in the order they were received. He can answer all at once. That is the God that we serve.

Roadside Assistance Scriptures

Don't be afraid, for I am with you. Don't be discouraged, for I am your God. I will strengthen you and help you. I will hold you up with my victorious right hand. (Isaiah 41:10)

For I hold you by your right hand I, the LORD your God. And I say to you, "Don't be afraid. I am here to help you." (Isaiah 41:13)

I cried out, "I am slipping!" but your unfailing love, O LORD, supported me.
When doubts filled my mind, your comfort gave me renewed hope and cheer. (Psalm 94:18–19)

I prayed to the LORD, and he answered me. He freed me from all my fears.

Those who look to him for help will be radiant with joy; no shadow of shame will darken their faces. (Psalm 34:4–5)

Taste and see that the LORD is good. Oh, the joys of those who take refuge in him! (Psalms 34:8)

Don't worry about anything; instead, pray about everything. Tell God what you need, and thank him for all he has done.

Then you will experience God's peace, which exceeds anything we can understand. His peace will guard your hearts and minds as you live in Christ Jesus. (Philippians 4:6–7)

CHAPTER 12

Arrived

Your towns and your fields will be blessed.
Your children and your crops will be blessed. The
offspring of your herds and flocks will be blessed.
Your fruit baskets and breadboards will be blessed.
Wherever you go and whatever you do, you will be blessed.

—Deuteronomy 28:3–6

It is a good feeling to finally arrive at your destination. I can remember many times when we left early. The directions took us straight to the place without an issue, and we were early. I can remember times when we had issues and arrived late. In the end, it felt good to finally be at the destination we were trying to reach.

The drive was over, and we were able to get out of the car and stretch out. Now, of course, the work began. We had to do what we were going to do at the destination. If it was a worship service we were going to, it was time to worship. If it was a doctor's appointment, it was time to be seen. If it was a meeting we were invited to, it was time to meet.

It is the same in our walk with Christ. He called us to start a ministry. We have followed all the instructions to the destination, and now it is time to do ministry. It is time for the work to begin. That first service can be a tough one. You are not sure if anyone is going to come. You are praying that you are in the right location. You don't want all your work to be in vain.

The same with a business. When those doors open for the first time, you are hoping and praying for customers to come and start spending money on your product or service. All the work you put into setting up everything was long and hard. You want it to pay off, and you want it to pay off quickly.

Now that you have arrived, you can't forget about the God Positioning System. You will still need direction through each stage of growth. When you first start out and there are only three kids in the nursery, it is not a big deal. You do nursery this Sunday, and I will do it next Sunday. If all else fails, just let the kids be with their parents that Sunday. But now that there are over twenty kids in the nursery each Sunday, you need to have a strategic plan.

Through it all, God's desire is to lead and guide His people because it is not just the nursery. Every area of the church will need to grow. Is there a plan to win the soul of that parent who only comes because they can get an hour-and-a-half break from the kids? God can give that plan. What about that single guy who only comes to hit on the sisters? Is there a plan to win that soul? God can give you the plan for that soul also.

When it was just a couple of teens, they sat in the sanctuary with their parents. Now parents are coming in with teens, and they want their teens to be in a solid youth program that teaches godly values and helps them grow in their relationship with Christ. What is your plan to win the souls of teens? God has a plan that will wins teens.

The husband who only comes so his wife will not be upset. He just wants peace in the home. What is the plan to win that husband? God has a plan for that.

One problem I see in the church is that we think, "It worked for that church, so let's try it here." We can't follow a plan that God gave someone else's ministry. We don't need copycat ministries. God placed you in a different community. Seek God, and let Him give you the right directions for the ministry and neighborhood He put you in.

What if my ministry is not a church but a nonprofit that provides for a need in the community? God can give you direction for your nonprofit. Now that you have arrived through obedience, now that the doors to your nonprofit are open, you will have opportunities to serve and minster to those who will never set foot in a church.

The Word of God makes some promises to those who are obedient. When you arrive at your destination, you can expect God to bless. Deuteronomy 28:3 says, "Your towns and your fields will be blessed." God was letting the Children of Israel know that when they walked in obedience, they would be blessed no matter where they were. These same words apply to us today. If God told you to plant a church on a country road, your obedience will be blessed. If God told you to plant a church in the middle of a city of two million, your obedience will be blessed.

The same for nonprofit and for-profit businesses. When the business is out of obedience to God, it will be blessed. As long as you have put the business in the place where God told you to put it, it will be blessed. Be obedient and go where God directs you to go; you will reap blessing when you get there. He can give you a plan to win the soul of that teenage mom. He can give you a plan to win the soul of that person coming to get food for their family.

You may think your nonprofit is just for that natural need you supply, but God can take your nonprofit and meet the spiritual needs of those who come in for your services. He just needs a willing vessel. Every time someone walks into your nonprofit, just say, "Use me, Lord." When they come through those doors, utter the words, "Help me, Holy Spirit." God will use you to save the souls of the lost.

What if my business is a for-profit business? The people who come in don't have financial issues. The people who come in seem to have it all together. People who are struggling in this life may want to know about Jesus. People who seem to have all they need and more don't seem to want anything to do with Jesus. The problem with this perspective is this: we only know what they look like on the outside. The God that we serve knows what they are dealing with deep down in their heart. He knows their every thought. God can give you the right words to say to win the rich, the poor, and everyone in between.

It would be great if someone came into your business to get some business advice and walked out filled with the Holy Spirit. How wonderful it would be if someone came into your business to get a new blouse, new pants, or new shoes, and walked out with the clothes and a word from the Lord. The God Positioning System will put us on the soul-winning road. All we have to do is follow the directions. Just put it into the GPS: "I want to win a soul today." Then wait for the instructions.

Whatever God has called us to do, know that it is kingdom business. Not all ministry takes place inside the four walls of a building we call the church. Ministry is defined as "of those who by the command of God proclaim and promote religion among men." Anytime we are promoting God in this world, we are doing ministry. Anytime we are testifying to the goodness of God, we are doing ministry.

Ministry is also defined as the ministration of those who render to others the offices of Christian affection, those who help meet needs by either collecting or distributing charities. When we are showing love, we are doing ministry. When we are helping those who are in need, we are doing ministry. This is more than just once a week on Sunday. We must be ready for ministry whenever God wants to use us.

If we have love in our heart and a desire to serve God and others, we can do ministry. Anyplace, anytime. Not saying we will never be rejected by man, but we will not be rejected by God. Many times, we are rejected by man because we are not being used by God; we are simply doing what someone told us we should do. Trust the God Positioning System and let God cause you to be a winner of souls.

I'm not saying there won't be tests and trials along the way, but there will be blessing as you go forth. Deuteronomy 28:4 says, "Your children and your crops will be blessed. The offspring of your herds and flocks will be blessed." First, this verse talks about blessing our children. When we walk in obedience to God, we cause our children to be blessed. When we think about the way the world is changing, our kids need the blessing of the Lord.

Our kids need God and divine protection. There is so much wickedness in this world today. They need divine protection as they go to school, grocery stores, movie theaters, in their cars, in their homes, and even church. All we need to do is look at the news to see what is happening in the world. This world has changed since I was born in 1972.

Our kids need God to move in the midst of their finances. Minimum-wage jobs are fine, but we should want more for children. Why can't they have the hundred-thousand-dollar-a-year jobs? Why can't our kids have a multimillion-dollar-a-year business? Then there is health and strength. Our kids should be healthy and full of joy. Lord, help our kids to eat right and exercise. The Word of God promised that if we are obedient, our kids will be blessed. Stand on the promise.

The next promise in verse 4 is that our crops would be blessed. I have eleven sisters and brothers, and not one of us is a farmer. We don't plant crops, but we can pray for those who do. Those who plant crops and are obedient will reap a harvest of blessings. Farmers, be obedient and reap the harvest.

The last part of verse 4 says, "The offspring of your herds and flocks will be blessed." This tells us that not only will our children be blessed but we have a blessing through the offspring of our herds and flocks. Once again, none of my siblings have herds and flocks. How does this apply to us?

I believe this: that whenever we plant a good word into someone's heart, we will reap the blessing. When we speak life into somebody, we reap the blessing. We may not plant natural seeds, but we will reap the harvest of the spiritual seeds we plant. We may not keep herds and flocks, but we do have jobs. God will pour out blessing and favor on us at our jobs. All we have to do is be obedient to the directions that He gives. Be obedient to the call.

Deuteronomy 28:5 says, "Your fruit baskets and breadboards will be blessed." Fruit baskets and breadboards were the way they carried their provisions. Nowadays, we have wallets, purses, and bank accounts, just to name a few. I can't speak for anyone else on this one, but I can say this. Whatever provisions my wife and I need, the Lord ensures we have what we need to get them.

When we need to go to the fruit basket, we find that the fruit basket is blessed. When we need to go to the breadboard, we find that the breadboard is full of blessings.

Some people came out and looked at the furnace a little while ago. They said it was old and needed to be replace. It was not working anymore, and wintertime was on the way. We went to the fruit basket. God had provisions in the fruit basket. We didn't need to use a credit card; God provides. They came back and said the water heater was on its way out. It was old and needed to be replaced. We went to the breadboard. We found that God had everything we needed in the breadboard. Once again, there was no need to charge it on a credit card. God had all that we needed in the breadboard.

Then the furnace went out in one of our rental properties. Don't you know, God had the provisions we needed. We can go to the fruit basket or the breadboard, and the provisions we need are there. Let me just give God some praise here. He provided so much that the fruit basket and the breadboard are still not empty. That's why nobody can stop my praise. God is true to His Word. Obedience leads to blessings. I believe that we have seen God do so many great things in our life, but we still we have not seen the best God has for us.

When we operate by the leading and guidance of the God Positioning System, it is as Deuteronomy 28:6 says: "Wherever you go and whatever you do, you will be blessed." God cannot lie. Through obedience, we will be blessed. How can God say that we will be blessed wherever we go and whatever we do? How can He make that promise to us? The reason God can say that is because when we are moving in obedience, we are in the place where He has told us to go, and we are doing what He told us to do.

These promises are dependent on our obedience to what God gives us instruction to do. We will not be blessed anyplace we go and whatever we do when we are not being obedient to God. Deuteronomy 28:1–2 says, "If you fully obey the LORD your God and carefully keep all his commands that I am giving you today, the LORD your God will set you high above all the nations of the world.

You will experience all these blessings if you obey the LORD your God."

Matthew 22:37–38 says, "You must love the LORD your God with all your heart, all your soul, and all your mind. This is the first and greatest commandment." When we love the Lord with all our heart, soul, and mind, we will have a desire to do His will. We will have a desire to see others come to Him. We will want to see others know the love of Christ even more than we know the love of Christ. We will walk in our calling to see others saved and grow in Christ just as we had to grow, and we are still growing. We will want to see others walk in their calling.

Jeremiah 17:10 says, "But I, the LORD, search all hearts and examine secret motives. I give all people their due rewards, according to what their actions deserve." When we walk in our calling, and when our motives are pure, I believe God will shower blessings, grace, and favor on us. Just like the prophet Jeremiah, our ministry may be rejected and contradicted by men, but if we continue in the Lord, we will get our due rewards. Lord, search our hearts and our motives. See if You find anything that is right in Your sight. We want to have a pure heart and pure motives before You.

Psalms 26:2 says, "Put me on trial, LORD, and cross-examine me. Test my motives and my heart." How do we get to a place where we can ask the Lord to put us on trial? How do we get to a place where we are so confident in the God in us, that we are willing to say to Him, "Cross-examine my motives"? "I want a ministry that is all about giving You the glory and honor, and not about me being lifted up. Look inside my heart, Jesus, where You reside. Show me how to lift You up in every area of my life."

My brothers and sisters, we have a God who will lead and guide us all along the way. It may not be where we want to go, and it may not be what we want to do. However, if we just trust the God Positioning System, we will reap the blessing of God. We have arrived, and now it is time to do the work.

ABOUT THE AUTHOR

L eroy Banks is a man of faith, a copastor of Kingdom Assignment Ministries in Bremerton, Washington, and founder of Walking in His Grace and Mercy (on Facebook and YouTube). He is a husband, father of three, and grandfather of nine. He was born in Denmark, South Carolina, where he lived until he joined the US navy in 1990. In 1995, he was stationed in Bremerton, Washington. He was filled with the Holy Spirit in December on 1996. It was in Bremerton where he met his wife, who was raised in Chula Vista, California. They were married in June of 1997.

Over the years, Banks served in different areas of the church. He was an usher, deacon, Brotherhood Department chair, minister, elder, and member of the pastoral leadership team. Now he serves at Kingdom Assignment Ministries, where people believe God to do great and mighty acts. They can see the cloud the size of a man's hand and are ready for the rain. The ministry is growing and thriving, walking by faith. Walking in His grace and mercy is an online teaching that Banks does each week. The goal is to provide practical teaching that will help those who watch draw closer to Christ, to see souls come to repentance, be baptized in Jesus's name, and be filled with the Holy Spirit. To see lives changed. None of this can happen without the leading of the Holy Spirit.

God gave him this book back in 2019. It took some time to bring it to fruition, but God never let him forget it. Here a little, there a little, over time. He continued to speak to the author. Leroy Banks prays that *The God Positioning System* will be a blessing to all who read it. He prays that lives will be changed.